Refined
in the
Furnace of Affliction

Rus –
Thanks for your friendship

John F. McCulloch

John McCulloch

Outskirts Press, Inc.
Denver, Colorado

CONTENTS

Acknowledgements v
Foreword vii
Introduction ix
The Navy 1
Johnny Gets Sick, Move to Bozeman 15
    and on to University
Livingston and Belt Creek 27
Stanford Montana...37
Bozeman...41
Gallatin Ranger District 57
Johnny and School 63
Bruce 71
Move to Big Timber..77
Johnny's Accident 85
Retirement 93
ALS 103
Epilogue 111
Photographs..115

ACKNOWLEDGEMENTS

I wish to acknowledge the help I received in writing this book. My daughter, Beverly, and sons Bruce and Bryan helped with facts, dates and recalling incidents that I had forgotten. Bruce actually wrote Chapter 8. Without their help, this would never have happened.

Others who read the first draft and offered suggestions were Jacquie Anderson, Tony and Ann Knick, Corey and Patti Heumier, Chris Blackmore, and Rose Clevidence. Their suggestions and ideas were invaluable.

I want to thank Gene Monson and Claudia LeCoure for their help and advice.

I have trouble finding the words to express my gratitude to Kathy Tyers, who has been writing and publishing books for many years. She completely edited the manuscript and gave me valuable advice.

Finally, I want to thank my wife, Janet, who read the manuscript and corrected much of my poor punctuation and word usage. I also want to thank her for her patience with me and putting up with my obsession to get the book done, resulting in long hours at the computer.

FOREWORD

I have been John's pastor during the majority of years that are covered in this book. We have both wept and rejoiced together on many occasions. So I can give a first hand confirmation of how he has responded to the challenges he has faced.

It is a true statement that "Trials can make us bitter or better." This book records some very difficult trials. I can declare that the results of these trials in John's life have lead to the "better". These trials have resulted in his being conformed more closely to the image of Christ. The Bible declares: **"And we know that in all things God works for the good of those who love him, who have been called according to his purpose. For those God foreknew he also predestined to be conformed the the likeness of his Son."** Romans 8:28-29a (New International Version).

Enjoy the autobiographical sketches, but don't miss the underlying truth of James 1:2-4 because John's experiences demonstrate its reality.

"Consider it pure joy, my brothers, whenever you face trials of many kinds, because you know that the testing of your faith developes perseverance. Perseverance must finish its work so that you may be

mature and complete, not lacking anything.” James 1:2-4 (NIV).

> Chris N. Blackmore, Pastor Emeritus,
> Evangelical Free Church of Bozeman,
> MT

INTRODUCTION

My purpose in writing this book is to encourage readers who are experiencing trouble to put their faith in the Lord, and trust Him to see them through the trial. This is true no matter how devastating, how heartbreaking, how seemingly unfair the affliction. Take the attitude of Job, who in the middle of losing his children, his servants, his crops, his livestock, his herdsmen, his home, being covered with painful sores, and having his wife tell him to curse God, made the following statement. "Though God slay me, still I will hope in Him." (Job 13:15)

We live in a fallen world. All of us are hit from time to time with tragedy. God allows this because Satan is the ruler of this world, but God has a way of turning tragedy around for our good. (Romans 8:28)

This book is the story of my family's experiences with affliction and how God used these experiences to draw us to Himself. I would be interested in your comments after reading the book. You may e-mail me at the following address:

John F. McCulloch
oldcoot69@earthlink.net

CHAPTER 1
THE NAVY

It was approximately 2:00 a.m. Sunday morning, December 13, 1957. I was asleep in my room in the Bachelor Officer's Quarters (BOQ) at the Naval Air Station, Sangley Point, Philippines. Someone was calling my name. "Mister McCulloch, Mister McCulloch, wake up!" I looked up to see the Filipino orderly. "Mister McCulloch, you have an urgent message at the Message Center."

I rolled out of my bunk and got dressed, wondering if my family was OK. I made my way to the Administration building that housed the communications center. The yeoman on duty asked to see my identification and handed me a telegram from my mother-in-law. It read something like this: "You are the father of a baby boy; however, there is something wrong and he is not expected to live. Please come home immediately." I thought, "This is awful. Mother doesn't understand the Navy. I think you have to confirm these things with the Red Cross or something. I will need to call and get more information. Where do I start?"

I was a lieutenant junior grade, flying seaplanes with Patrol Squadron Forty-Two based at Sangley Point, a peninsula jutting into Manila Bay and a thirty-minute boat ride from the capital of the Philippine Islands.

I walked slowly back to the BOQ, wondering what to do about the message. I was very concerned for my wife Sylvia, and I wondered if she was all right. When I arrived at the barracks, I sat down in an easy chair in the lounge and stewed about my situation. To phone Sylvia in Alabama, I would have to go into Cavite—the nearest town—and it was too early. After four frustrating hours, the Skipper came down on his way to Manila to play golf. "What are you doing up, Mac?" he asked. I showed him the message. He told me to wake up the Personnel Officer and have him cut orders for Emergency Leave.

Bob Lefevre, the Assistant Personnel Officer, was one of my roommates. I woke him up, showed him the message and told him what the Skipper had said. Together, Bob and I walked to the Administration Office near the seaplane ramp. Bob typed up the orders, made about three extra copies, and told me to call Operations to see when the next plane was leaving for the States.

When I phoned Operations, I learned there was a plane leaving for the U.S. that morning. I packed up my belongings and put on my winter (Blue) uniform, as it was December and I figured we would be going straight through to San Francisco. After showing my orders and getting them endorsed, I boarded the plane. There were only a few passengers.

We flew to Guam, where the pilot announced there would be a twenty-four hour crew rest. I was amazed. "Can I get my suitcase?" I asked the plane captain. He answered,

"No way. Everything is stowed in the baggage compartment. You should have put some stuff in a carry-on bag."

I was devastated, to say the least. On my way to the Navy Exchange to pick up some toilet articles, a sailor saluted and said, "Man, I haven't seen Blues for three years. Aren't you hot?" I was sweating, all right. At the Exchange, I bought a book and some other things, then walked to the BOQ. I got a room, stripped to my underwear and spent the day trying to read, but it was hard to concentrate on a book. My mind was on my wife and new son.

The next morning, we continued the flight to Barber's Point, Hawaii. On the way, another officer suggested I volunteer for courier duty for the rest of the trip, since everyone was flying on Emergency Leave at Christmas time, and all flights were likely to be full. When we reached Barber's Point, I told the plane captain I was leaving the flight and needed my suitcase. He got it for me, and somehow I made it to the Air Force Base at Hickam Field. At the Operations Office, I told the sergeant at the desk I wanted to volunteer for courier duty, and he told me to have a seat. In a little while, my name was called. I was told to board an Air Force cargo plane, maybe a C-4, large enough to carry a couple of tanks. A Navy Chief Petty Officer got on with me.

While waiting to be called for courier duty, I had phoned my wife and learned that my son, John Ewalt McCulloch, had been injured during birth. They had given Sylvia a drug, Scopolamine, that she was allergic to. She had thrashed around on the table during the birth process, and the baby sustained a head injury. He had been placed in an incubator for a time but was stable now; however, he had come down with chickenpox. I thought, "What next?"

We taxied out to the edge of the runway and stopped. An Air Police van with a red light drove up to the plane. An Air Policeman came on board and handcuffed a briefcase to me, then issued the Chief a .45-caliber automatic pistol. After the policeman left, we took off immediately. The Chief and I pulled a couple of stretchers off the bulkhead and found a couple of blankets, so we could try and sleep on the flight to Travis Air Force Base, East of San Francisco.

The flight was routine. When we landed at Travis, we taxied off the duty runway and stopped. Another Air Police truck drove up to the plane. Two more armed Air Policeman came on board, un-cuffed the briefcase and took the .45 from the Chief, and left. We taxied to the Operations building and got off the plane.

At Travis Air Operations, there was a board listing departing flights from the area. A flight was leaving for Pensacola, Florida, the next morning from the Naval Air Station at Oakland. I borrowed a phone and called the Air Station. Yes, there was a Naval Reserve flight going to Pensacola. Yes, I could get on the flight.

I walked out of the operations front entrance and found a taxicab parked at the curb. The driver said he was available, and I told him to take me to the Naval Air Station at Oakland, roughly 50 miles. Graciously, he reached up and shut off the meter.

At the Air Station, I paid him $20 and went to Operations. N.A.S. Oakland is a Naval Reserve base. The yeoman inside was very friendly, and he asked to see my orders. "My gosh, you only have two copies of your orders? You will need more copies. I'll make you some." He took the original and made me several more copies. "You're on board for tomorrow morning," he said, and then he directed me to the Bachelor Officer's Quarters and told me where to get something to eat.

The next morning, I boarded a Navy transport piloted by Naval Reserve pilots, getting in their reserve hours. The plane was going to Pensacola to pick up naval cadets from the area, to bring them home for Christmas.

It was snowing and very cold when we landed in Albuquerque, NM, where we re-fueled and took off on the last leg for Pensacola. When we hit Louisiana, it began to rain. It was dark out, but the sky outside the cabin window was lit up with lightning, and the plane bounced around. We landed safely but very late at Sherman Field, N.A.S. Pensacola. I went to the BOQ and went to bed. I didn't sleep very well and was up early. I took a taxi to the bus depot and rode the bus to Mobile, Alabama, where I met Sylvia and our new son.

Johnny was still in Providence Hospital. They wanted to keep him a little longer to be sure he was OK, and Sylvia had to stay with him. It was great to see her; she hugged me and hung on like she wasn't going to let me go. While we waited for Johnny to be released, my mother-in-law took me to Bayou La Batre to show me around. Sylvia had recently purchased a 1957 Ford with money I had sent home, so I had wheels. I had told her to get the best deal she could, and that we could probably get a better deal on the 1957 models because the '58s were in stock.

Sylvia's mother took me to meet Floyd and Fannie, friends who had helped Sylvia pick out the car. When we got to Floyd and Fannie's, they were in the kitchen bottling moonshine, of all things. After introductions, they handed me a jelly glass (about 2 1/2 shots) of the liquor. It was clearer than any water I'd ever seen. In those days, I had been known to take a drink. I tossed off the whole glassful. It seemed like it stuck in my throat and burned, then continued burning down my esophagus into my stomach. "Isn't that the best stuff you've ever drank?" Floyd asked. I nodded in the affirmative because I couldn't speak for a moment. I assured them it was good but refused a second glass.

On Christmas day, Sylvia's mother cooked turkey, ham, sweet potato pie and fresh fried oysters, along with cornbread dressing, potatoes and gravy, sweet potatoes and more. Johnny seemed to be doing OK, so they had sent him home at last. Sylvia and I had only been married a year when my squadron deployed to the Philippines, and it was great to be with my wife. It was strange to be a father, though. Johnny was a cute little guy, and Sylvia was a good mother. Unfortunately, the time passed too quickly. It was soon time to return to duty.

Sylvia and I had only known each other for six months before I went to Corpus Christi, Texas for advanced training. She was a student nurse at Providence Hospital in Mobile, Alabama, and ours was a whirlwind courtship. One weeknight I came to the nurses' residence to take the girl I was dating, Jewel, for coffee. Her roommate Sylvia came down and told me Jewel had to work at the hospital for another girl, who was sick. Sylvia and I had met before, at a dance, but we didn't really know each other. Somehow she looked really good that night, and I went back to the base at Barin Field, near Foley, Alabama, thinking about her and remembering that dance. The student nurses would put on dances at their residence, and they invited the Navy cadets to attend. To this day, I tell people I met Sylvia at a nursing home dance. One of my friends said, "Wow! You were a real rounder, McCulloch." I guess you don't call nurses' residences "nursing homes."

A couple of days later, I went to the nurses' quarters and asked for Sylvia. She had been dating a student from Spring Hill College, where the nursing students took their academic classes. He was also named John, and when the girl at the desk told her "John" was waiting to see her, she sent a friend to see who it was, as she was mad at the other John. When she found out it was me, she was surprised, but she consented to go with me for coffee. I took her home and asked her for another date on the following Saturday, which she accepted.

The next Saturday was Mardi Gras in Mobile. Mobile's celebration before Lent is older than the one in New Orleans but not as well known. The student nurses helped by manning first aid stations in downtown Mobile, and I picked Sylvia up at the aid station where she was working. She was in her nursing uniform and had left her change of clothes in a hearse they were using for a substitute ambulance. The hearse had been called out to pick up a body, so our first order of business was to find Sylvia's clothes. They had gone with the hearse to a funeral home, where she went inside and changed. We spent the rest of the evening at a carnival and had a great time together.

After that, we saw each other every time I could get off the base. One time when I was stationed at Corey Field, I buzzed the hospital in a T-28 trainer, trying to get her attention. It turned out she was oblivious to it, but if I had been caught, I would have been in serious trouble. What can I say?...I was in love!

Before I left for Corpus Christi to begin advanced training in seaplanes, I asked Sylvia to marry me. We had known each other only four months. For the next two months, we corresponded by letter and telephone.

We were married September 13, 1956, in Sylvia's hometown of Camden, Arkansas at the First Baptist Church. My parents and two younger brothers came in from Montana. We had a couple of days to wait before the wedding, and Sylvia showed me around Camden. I had a 1952 Chevrolet convertible at the time, and we were driving around town with the top down. As we drove up one residential street, an older man was working in his yard, and when he saw us he hollered, "Hey!" and motioned for us to come over. I asked Sylvia if she knew him, and when she acknowledged that she did, I stopped. He came to the car and without introductions said, "Where are you from, boy?" I answered, "Montana." He said, "What church do you go to?" I replied, "The Christian Church." He said, "Never heard of it, but let me tell you something, boy. You take care of her or we'll come and get you." I think he was trying to scare me, but it could've been just Southern humor.

We honeymooned in Montana and Yellowstone Park,

and then we finally left for San Diego, California. My duty station was to be at North Island Naval Air Station, just outside Coronado and across the bay from San Diego. We had a wonderful year together before I left for the Philippines.

Picking up the story in Mobile at Christmas 1957, my orders were for a thirty-day leave. After that, I was to report to Fleet Air Service Squadron, San Diego and wait for my squadron to return. A few days before my leave was up, I took our new car and drove to California. Sylvia was going to stay in Alabama with our new baby for a while and fly out later. I met up with an old high school friend, Marty Slagle, in Wichita Falls, TX. He was in the Army, stationed at Fort Sill, OK. He invited me to spend the night with him and his wife in Lawton, OK. A couple of nights later, I stayed with another friend, Nevin Thompson, a dentist in the Air Force, based in Tucson, AZ. We did a lot of visiting and I didn't sleep much, and consequently, when I got to San Diego, I came down with mononucleosis. I didn't have any duty assignments, so I stayed in my room at BOQ and slept—except that I did take time to find an apartment and purchase a baby crib.

I was only in San Diego a few days when I received orders to return to the Philippines via Military Air Transport Service (MATS). We landed at Clark A.F.B., and I caught a Grumman amphibian mail plane to Sangley Point. When I landed, I was met by some of my buddies and was told the Acting Executive Officer wanted to see me.

Patrol Squadron VP-40 was supposed to relieve us, but due to head winds, they had been unable to leave San

Francisco for over thirty days. The P5M seaplane did not have a lot of range. The first leg from San Francisco to Hawaii was the longest stretch in the trans-Pacific flight, and the Navy required a two-hour fuel reserve at our destination, so any amount of head wind along the way would justify postponing the flight. We had twelve aircraft in our squadron, and every aircraft required a crew of three and sometimes four: first pilot, co-pilot, and one or two navigators. This meant that there needed to be a minimum of 36 pilots to get the twelve planes home. Since our relieving squadron, VP-40, was delayed in relieving us, many of our people were receiving orders to new duty stations or being released from active duty; therefore, they sent for me.

I reported to the Acting Executive Officer, who proceeded to ask if I had gone home because my son contracted chickenpox. I assured him that was not the reason, but he then told me I had not gone through the chain of command when I got my orders home, and so he was ordering me to do a twenty-four hour watch as Crash Boat Duty officer. The Crash Boat was responsible for sweeping the sea lane that the pilots used for take-offs and landings, and the man on Crash Boat duty had to be ready to deal with any emergency in seaplane traffic. It wouldn't have been bad (I had stood that duty many times), but this time, I was still sick with mononucleosis. I took my bag to the barracks, changed uniforms, and reported as ordered.

I don't know how I got through the twenty-four hour watch. When I went to dinner after getting off duty, our flight surgeon, Lt. Bill Anthony, took one look at me and sent me to the hospital. I had a high fever and was very sick.

As I remember, I spent about ten days in the hospital . When I got out, the Skipper—who had been our Executive Officer—had apparently found out the real reason for my emergency leave. He evidently felt some guilt, because he ordered me to go on "Rest and Rehabilitation" to Hong Kong. He sent Lt. Anthony and VP-40's flight surgeon to accompany me.

I had been to Japan, but never to Hong Kong. When we landed, a British officer met the plane and briefed us about the Hong Kong Chinese. He told us to put our wallets in our front pants pocket and keep our hand in the pocket, over our wallet, at all times when walking on the streets. It was a brief but interesting visit. I remember Hong Kong as teeming with people, like leaving a football game everywhere we went.

When I returned to Sangley Point, I flew one patrol before we were ordered to fly home on Navy transports and trade aircraft with VP-40. Our Skipper protested, but to no avail.

When we arrived at North Island N.A.S. in San Diego, Sylvia came to meet the plane. Boy, it was good to be home and see her again. We settled into our new apartment. I wasn't there very long before I applied for and got thirty days' leave to visit my folks in Bozeman, Montana. My grandmother was still living, then. She was a "snowbird," spending winters in Long Beach but heading back to Bozeman in the summer months. It was early for her, but she decided to go to Montana with Sylvia and me.

When we arrived to pick up Grandma, she wasn't quite finished packing, so Sylvia and I helped her get her things together. I remember she emptied about a teaspoonful of salt out of a salt shaker onto a piece of wax paper, tied it up with a rubber band and put it in her suitcase. I commented, "Grandma, you can get a whole box of salt for about ten cents." Embarrassed, she explained that she had lived through tough times in the Great Depression and had formed these habits. We let it go. She also complained about the price we paid for motels on the way home. All in all, though, it was a good trip.

Unfortunately, while we were in Bozeman, Johnny got sick again. His head started to grow, a condition called hydrocephalus. We took Johnny to my dad's doctor, who told us he couldn't help us physically but would refer us to the best neurosurgeon he knew of, at the University of California Medical School in San Francisco. He said, "If anything can be done, they can do it. If they can't do anything," he added, "put John in an institution and don't spend any more money, and by all means, have more children."

This was pretty tough to take. To say the least, we were devastated. We decided to leave for San Francisco right away. The only thing I remember about the trip was a terrific snow storm on Donner Pass, where even a train was snowbound. We avoided the pass by taking U.S. 70 North to get across the mountains.

When we got to San Francisco, we went immediately to the Medical Center, but we couldn't see the doctor until the next day. We left Johnny at the hospital and spent the night in a cheap hotel nearby. I'm sure Sylvia was doing a good deal of praying, but I didn't really have a relationship with the Lord at that time. I was just in a state of shock.

The next morning, we met with the neurosurgeon. He had been head of neurosurgery at the University of California Medical School, but he was retired. I don't recall his name, but he referred us to his successor, Dr. John Adams. After a thorough examination, Dr. Adams operated and placed a shunt from Johnny's spinal column into his stomach, to drain the spinal fluid and allow the head to grow normally. The absorption pads in Johnny's brain had been injured at birth, and scar tissue had formed over the injured area, blocking the normal absorption of fluid, causing hydrocephalus. The purpose of the shunt was to relieve the pressure until the absorption pads healed naturally.

I stayed with Sylvia until my leave was up. We found a boarding house across the street from the hospital and got Sylvia settled there. Then I took the car and drove to North Island, San Diego and reported for duty. The squadron was in a training mode, with new people reporting in all the time. We had a new Executive Officer, and some other pilots were just out of flight training.

The next weekend, I drove to San Francisco to see my family. Johnny's surgery was declared a success, and Sylvia soon took him home to our apartment in Coronado, just outside the North Island Naval Air Station.

CHAPTER 2
JOHNNY GETS SICK, MOVE TO
BOZEMAN AND ON TO UNIVERSITY

Things went well for the next few months. On weekends, we took trips to Knotts Berry Farm, Mount Palomar, Disneyland, Tijuana, and spent a lot of time at Balboa Park. My Air Force friend Nevin Thompson and his wife Norma came one weekend, and we went sightseeing around the San Diego area.

When Johnny was seven months old, he began to get sick again. He would throw up, and again his head began to enlarge. The Navy had made a new ruling that we couldn't go to civilian doctors if there were Navy medical facilities available. Balboa Naval Hospital in San Diego was one of the largest medical facilities in the Navy, so we took Johnny there and checked him in. The neurosurgeon, a Navy captain, put dye in Johnny's back and x-rayed him. He told us that Johnny had communicating hydrocephalus, which we already knew. We left the baby in the hospital for two weeks. Sylvia, who had two years of nurses' training, camped at the hospital. One day, I got a phone call at the squadron. Sylvia was crying. "They are not doing anything for Johnny," she said. I told her I would be right over. I got permission to leave and went to the hospital. We picked up the baby and walked out. We didn't even check him out, that I remember.

We got in the car and drove to San Francisco. Dr. Adams was furious and made no bones about it. "He's lost his eyesight," he announced. "What did they do at the Navy hospital?" Unfortunately, the Navy doctor didn't know anything about Johnny's condition but was too proud to admit it. He could have waived the rules and released us to go to the California Medical Center. As it turned out, Johnny was made a patient of the medical school. This was fortunate, not only for financial reasons, but because we had a steady stream of student doctors looking in on Johnny and asking us questions. This made the time pass faster, and it helped us deal with our guilt feelings and extreme stress. Dr. Adams operated and freed up the shunt, which had plugged.

For the next year, I continued to fly and work in the squadron supply shop. I qualified as Aircraft Commander, 1st pilot. The Navy tried hard to get me to re-enlist, but I didn't want to go back to the Philippines and leave Sylvia and Johnny, so when my active duty tour was up, I got a "Release From Active Duty" and we returned to Bozeman, Montana.

We were home about two months when Johnny's head began to enlarge again. Once again, he began to throw up. We learned there was a neurosurgeon in Billings, so I called to see if they would do a spinal tap on Johnny so we could take him back to California. The doctor in Billings, Dr. Baumann, said he could do anything there they could do in California, but if we wanted to go back to San Francisco, he would not get involved.

We felt we were between a rock and a hard place.

Sylvia prayed and I stewed, and we decided to take Johnny to Billings. It turned out to be a good decision. Dr. Baumann removed one of the baby's kidneys and placed the shunt into the sterile kidney cavity. Johnny never had another problem with his hydrocephalus. However, the pressure had damaged the optic nerve. He was legally blind.

In Bozeman, I got a job with the U.S. Forest Service working on a land exchange. Later, I participated in a recreation inventory of the Gallatin National Forest. Our second son, Bryan, was born in April. In August, I was in the field a lot, staying in Forest Service guard stations. I was mostly home on weekends, so my parents helped Sylvia with the babies.

At 11:57 p.m. on August 17, 1959, the upper Madison Canyon near West Yellowstone was hit by an earthquake that registered 7.5 on the Richter Scale. I was in a Forest Service cabin on the Boulder River, south of Big Timber, Montana, approximately sixty air miles from the epicenter. The quake woke us up. Dirt and rocks were falling off the mountain across from where we were staying. The entire Boulder canyon was filled with dust.

We turned on the radio and learned that the epicenter was at the "Duck Creek Y" near West Yellowstone, but the shock was felt in Ennis and Bozeman and the surrounding area. I got on the phone and tried to call my wife. The operator asked if it was an emergency. I told her it was. I got Sylvia on the phone; she was fine. At that time, she was alone in my parents' home, in the upstairs apartment. When the earthquake hit, she grabbed a baby in each arm and went downstairs. Neighbors from across the street came over, and they drank coffee and listened to the news on the radio.

Twenty-eight people lost their lives in the earthquake. A mountain split in half and slid into the Madison River, forming a huge dam. People downstream were evacuated because the Corps of Engineers thought the new dam would give way and send a surge of water down the canyon, into the Madison River Valley. Engineers brought in drag lines and dozers to cut a channel in the dam before it broke on its own.

The next two summers, I worked in the Madison Canyon Earthquake Area, which was designated a National Geological Site. A visitor's center was built on the big earth slide.

In the fall of 1959, we moved to Missoula, Montana, where I enrolled in forestry at the University of Montana. I had taken three years of college, one of them in forestry, before I went into the Navy. We moved into married student housing, which consisted of WWII military surplus buildings. They were long and narrow, like barracks, with five apartments in each building. The wooden buildings were parallel, and the yard between them was closed in with a tall fence on both ends, so toddlers and small children could play in the yard and mothers didn't have to worry about the kids escaping. Our apartment had three bedrooms, and the rent was $37.50 per month. You could push on the flimsy flooring and see the ground beneath the building. My father helped me put down tar paper on the floor and cover it with old carpet. The entire apartment was heated by a single space heater.

We had unusually cold weather for Missoula that October, with cold Hellgate winds. I bought plastic sheeting and nailed it over the windows to help seal them. In the mornings, the shower drain would freeze. If I ran the hot water, the drain would usually thaw just before the water ran over the top of the shower sill. Sylvia would put snow-suits and overshoes on the kids so they could play on the floor of the apartment. The top half of the rooms would be hot, the floors cold. In the ten apartments in the two buildings that shared our common yard, there were nineteen kids, and three of the apartments were empty.

We got acquainted with all our neighbors. No one had any money, so we would often get together and play cards for entertainment. We would dial our home phone from the neighbors, take the phones off the hook and listen to see if any of the kids were crying.

Our first neighbors were from Canada, Jean and Jack Holmes. Jack was a graduate student in the Forestry School. He was a great help to me in getting through my courses, especially the first quarter. It had been four years since I was in school, and my study habits were rusty. Jack's graduate work was in Forest Soils. He finished at the end of Fall quarter. Winter quarter, the University hired Jack to teach Soil Science while the former professor took a teaching job in Missouri.

Jack had a little ornery streak. He bought a German Shepherd puppy, which was against the rules. Since the University needed him to teach, they ignored the infraction. Jack then tried to talk us into getting a dog for Johnny. He thought we could get a doctor's order and get around the University because of Johnny's blindness. We asked Johnny's doctor, and he thought it would be a good idea. He said that it was important for blind children to get used to dogs, because when they walked with a cane, dogs might bark at them. So we got Lucky, a German Shepherd-Chesapeake Retriever cross. We put up a woven wire fence in the front yard to let the dog out into. As the puppy grew, he decided that his place in the world was to protect Johnny, which he did aggressively, to our consternation. We ended up giving the dog to a farmer after a couple of years.

Johnny turned two years old during the December after we moved to Missoula. Because of his visual impairment, when he walked he had to hang on to something for security. He also had trouble with other skills, such as dressing himself. Our doctor recommended occupational therapy. Community Hospital had a Occupational Therapy program. The therapist, Louise Zern, was fantastic. Among other things, she taught Johnny how to tie his shoes. I was amazed. How do you teach a blind two-year-old to tie his shoes? Anyway, we were blessed and Louise won us over.

Jean and Jack were our neighbors for a year, and then they moved back to Canada. Jean taught Sylvia to knit heavy wool cardigan sweaters. The first one she made was white with a black buffalo on it. I still have it, along with one she made my father.

In the fall of 1960, Sharron and Archie Dudden moved into the apartment next door. They had a little girl, Lynn, who was about Bryan's age. We got acquainted right away and became good friends. Sylvia was pregnant with our third baby. We planned to have a joint Thanksgiving together. Sylvia was preparing the turkey on the morning of November 24, Thanksgiving day, when her water broke. I rushed her to the hospital, and she gave birth to our third son, Bruce Allan.

Bruce was a quiet baby, and because Johnny required a great deal of attention due to his blindness, and Bryan was aggressive and demanded attention, Bruce was easy to ignore. This may be part of the reason that later, we had difficulties with Bruce.

The single-bedroom apartment on the other side of us had been vacant for two years, and in the fall of 1960, a couple of newlyweds moved in. The walls were paper thin, and we could hear them laughing through our kitchen wall. The new couple was hard to get to know, as they kept to themselves. One early evening, we heard a lot of giggling and running next door and then a loud crash, followed by uncontrolled laughter. We knocked on the door and learned that the guy had been chasing his wife when she jumped on the bed, he followed, and the bed crashed to the floor. No one was hurt, but it broke the ice and we got to know them a little better.

Spring quarter of my senior year was spent at a logging camp near Libby, Montana. I came home on weekends but usually spent them studying or writing a term paper. Sylvia was busy caring for our three boys. She was good at making friends, however, and that helped her get through the days.

The summers of 1960 and 1961, I worked for the Gallatin National Forest at the earthquake area near West Yellowstone. I was an interpreter, or guide. The earthquake had occurred the year before, and Highway 287 had been flooded by a new lake, Earthquake Lake. Hundreds of visitors came those summers to hear the stories and view the mountain that slid into the Madison River. My mother and dad had property in West Yellowstone, so we stayed in a basement apartment in the larger of two cabins. The property was in the northeast corner of the city, with Yellowstone National Park on the east of the property and the Gallatin National Forest on the north.

One day, Bryan and our neighbor's boy, Scotty, rode their tricycles under the Park fence and out through the trees to an opening, where they got off their tricycles and began playing in the sand. Sylvia was in the apartment doing something with Johnny. When she went upstairs to check on the kids, they were gone. She and Scotty's mother looked and called, but they couldn't find the boys anywhere. In a panic, Sylvia called me at the Forest Service office, which was about 100 yards away. Bears were known to hang out in West Yellowstone. In fact, we had dealt with bears several times that summer. We got together a search party of Forest Service employees and neighbors and began searching the area. Scotty's cocker spaniel, who had gone with the boys, heard the calls and came out of the Park to see what the fuss was about. He led us to the boys, who were calmly playing in the sand. I guess they were far enough away they didn't hear us calling, or they chose to ignore us.

Another time, there was a forest fire near Baker's Hole Campground. The fire was man- caused by a careless camper, and although it began on the National Forest, the wind took it into the crowns of the lodgepole pine trees, and it jumped the Madison River into Yellowstone Park. I was called to be crew boss of a bunch of volunteers, some of whom were drunk. This was my first project fire, and it was quite an experience. There were three crews of 25 men to a sector. Our sector boss was Evan White, an old timer with the Forest Service. Evan lined us up in a long file and addressed the crews as follows: "Take a good look at the men on either side of you, and don't get out of line or you won't get paid." We used the "step up" method of building fire line. A scout went ahead and flagged the line. Next came chainsaws to clear away fallen logs. Next were pulaskis, a hand tool with a combination grub hoe and axe on the head. Then shovels and pulaskis alternately. When a man finished the section of line he was working on, he said, "bump," and the next one in line moved up and bumped the next man, etc.

We started building hand line, then bulldozers were brought in and made short work of controlling the fire. We mopped up with "Pacific Marine" pumps, which we used to draw water from the river. It took about a week to get the fire pretty well mopped up.

The Baker's Hole fire was good training for me. A short time later, I was sent to Donner Ridge, in California, as a crew boss for a much larger fire. This was the beginning of a Forest Service career that included many wildfires and controlled burns.

We had our dog Lucky with us in West Yellowstone. As I said earlier, he took it upon himself to protect Johnny. One day, my cousin Ralph Aaker came to visit. Ralph was a County Commissioner for Gallatin County. I was at work in the Earthquake area, Sylvia was home in our basement apartment with the kids, and Johnny was taking a nap. Ralph and Sylvia were visiting when Johnny, who was about three, got up and came out of the bedroom. Ralph stood up from his seat and said, "Johnny, how are you?" As he moved toward Johnny, Lucky jumped between them with the hair up on his back and his lips curled in a snarl. Sylvia grabbed the dog, and Ralph sat back down.

Another time, we took a trip into the Park with the kids and left Lucky behind. There were no leash laws, so we just let the dog run. My dad had decided to list the property for sale, and a realtor came by to check out the property. He went down the basement steps to put a note on our door, and when he turned around, Lucky was at the top of the steps with a snarl on his lips. The realtor had to get to his car, so he went up the stairs. Lucky grabbed his pant leg. He didn't get any flesh, but the man dragged the dog to his car. When he later told us about the incident, we decided we should get rid of the dog. I ended up giving him to a cousin, George Tate, who gave him to his sister-in-law on a ranch near Townsend. They made a cattle dog out of him, and he got a good home.

My senior year at the University of Montana was actually my sixth year of college. I'd had three years before I enlisted in the Navy, two at Montana State in Bozeman, and my freshman year in forestry at the university in Missoula. This was during the Korean War, and the draft was still on. I had been re-classified for the draft when I changed majors and universities, so to avoid being drafted, I had enlisted in the Navy.

Another forestry student, Tom Kovalicky, and I had started our freshman year together and then gone into the military for four years. We had the same advisor, who thought we needed to take freshman speech, a five-credit course. I had taken three-credit courses in public speaking and voice and diction at Montana State, but that didn't seem to matter. We were seniors and could see daylight, so to speak. We didn't want to mess up, so we sat in the front row and tried our best to be enthusiastic in a 1 p.m. freshman speech class. The teacher was a member of the John Birch Society and was paranoid about communism. She had us each make a scrapbook of news articles that appeared to favor the communist cause. I assigned my scrapbook to Sylvia, and she got me an A.

One day, I was worried about a test coming up and decided to skip speech to study for the test. The teacher asked Tom where I was, and he told her I was giving a speech to the Rotary Club. She thought that was wonderful. In truth, Tom didn't have a clue where I was. Why he said that, I don't know but, the next day before class, he took me aside and said, " If she says something strange to you, just go along with it, OK?" After class, he told me what he had told her.

CHAPTER 3
LIVINGSTON AND BELT CREEK

When I graduated in June of 1962, Sylvia was pregnant with our fourth baby. I had applied to the Forest Service for a career appointment, and got it. I was assigned to the Yellowstone Ranger District, Gallatin National Forest, headquartered in Livingston, Montana. The District Ranger was Clem Kalitowski, a great supervisor. Near the end of my first year and the Government fiscal year, Clem took leave and left me to balance the books. I remember I left a few dollars in every account. When he returned from leave he said, "You did OK, but you should have been a few dollars in the red in each account. The supervisor's office would cover it."

I had a lot to learn, but I had good teachers in Assistant Ranger Jim Jordan and Ranger Kalitowski. We shared an office with the Shields River Ranger District. We had two secretaries that worked for both districts. Kalitowski was their supervisor. We could always tell when the ranger had been dealing with disputes between the two girls, as his wastebasket would be full of un-smoked pipe tobacco. When Clem would get nervous, he had a habit of filling his pipe and shaking it out into the waste basket without lighting up.

I did a little of everything that summer. We read range transects, administered timber sales, marked timber for cutting and did "correction factor scaling." The latter was a procedure for determining the final volume of lumber in a timber sale. We used statistical sampling by randomly selecting cruise plots to estimate the timber volume before selling it. We would seek out the selected plots and fell the timber, cut it into logs, scale it and record the defect, comparing the actual results with the original estimate and then adjusting the volume estimate accordingly. The result would be the figure used for the final price of the timber. Much of this scaling was done in the winter, on snowshoes.

On November 15, 1962, Jim Jordan and I were inspecting a timber sale in Mill Creek, south of Livingston. When we returned to the truck, I checked in on the radio. Our secretary asked if Jim Larkin had gotten in touch with me. When I answered, "no," she told me Sylvia had gone into labor. Our other secretary was on the phone to our home, and the girls were giving a blow-by-blow description of Sylvia's labor pains. To reach us on the air, they had to use the radio repeater, so the transmissions went to all seven ranger districts, as well as the Supervisor's office. Jim, a bachelor, drove us out of the mountains at an uncomfortable speed. He went around switchbacks and down the logging road like it was his wife. I assured him I had gone through this before and it wasn't that big a crisis.

When we got to our home in Livingston, several of our friends and neighbors were there. We had to park half a block away. They had Sylvia in one car and her suitcase in another, and they were getting ready to take her to Bozeman to have the baby. We got everything sorted out and into our own car and left for the hospital. Our friends had alerted the Bozeman hospital, but when we arrived, Sylvia decided she was not ready yet and suggested we go to my parents' home for coffee, which we did. The hospital called the Montana Highway Patrol and told them there was a lady having a baby somewhere between Bozeman and Livingston, a 25-mile stretch of highway.

When Sylvia was ready, we drove across Bozeman to the hospital and she gave birth to our daughter, Beverly. Since we had three boys, I asked the doctor if he was sure it was a girl. He assured me he knew the difference. Then he scolded me for waiting so long and stirring up such a ruckus. I was so excited over my new daughter that I let it pass, but felt I was the victim of circumstances.

That Christmas, Clem, whose hobby was woodworking, cut up a cardboard box full of various shaped wooden blocks and brought it to the boys. They were better than any blocks you could buy, and we had them for years. I may still have some of them. It was one of the best toys the kids ever had. When they got them out, however, there were so many blocks that it made quite a mess on the living room floor of our little apartment.

The next year, Jim Jordan was transferred and Bill and Hazel Pederson came to the district. We became good friends. Bill and I put up a huge timber sale, fought fires and went fishing together.

One day, I came home from several days in the field, where we stayed in guard stations (cabins) to be closer to our work. Sylvia said to hurry and shower and get dressed, as we were going to a school board meeting. She had tried to enroll Johnny in kindergarten and was turned down. The school principal said they weren't equipped to deal with a blind student. Sylvia was pretty even-tempered, except when someone was unfair to her children. She had phoned the Governor's office and been referred to the Superintendent of Public Instruction. A representative of the Superintendent was coming to the board meeting that night. As a result of Sylvia's efforts, the board accepted Johnny in kindergarten. His teacher, Mrs. Vasichek, became one of Johnny's champions. She was wonderful, and the Superintendent had a complete change of heart. Later, he bragged about Johnny. Mrs Vasichek stayed in touch with us for several years.

Since Johnny would need to attend first grade at the School for the Blind in Great Falls, Montana, I requested a transfer to the Lewis and Clark National Forest, to be closer to his school. In June of 1964, we were transferred to the Belt Creek Ranger District near Neihart, Montana. Carl Marsh was the District Ranger. That year, there was an early spring rain on an unusually large snow pack, resulting in bad flooding in the Rocky Mountain front near Augusta and Choteau. The Assistant Ranger, Jim Fishburn, had been detailed to the flood area, so I had plenty to do. My main job was in timber management, however. The ranger asked me if I could ski. I told him I had messed around with skis when I was younger, but was not really a skier. He said, "We will give you lessons. You are the new Snow Ranger at the King's Hill ski area."

In the fall, Johnny started first grade at the School for the Deaf and Blind, which was a boarding school. It was heartbreaking to leave Johnny that first day. I don't remember how we dealt with the first week, but when

Friday came, we were at the school early to pick him up and bring him home for the weekend. The logic behind Montana's decision to combine the deaf and blind schools escapes me. A deaf child and a blind child have no way of communicating, so the school had to keep the students separated.

My father was representing Gallatin County in the Montana Legislature. He sponsored a bill to increase funding for the School, and he brought Johnny to Helena to help promote his efforts. The bill passed.

Each weekend, we would get Johnny on Friday night and take him back to the school on Sunday evening. The trip was 50 miles one way. When it was just Johnny and me, we would sing, and I would teach him goofy songs and some of the oldies. Johnny already loved to sing. It was always hard to leave him on Sunday night, especially the first year, when he was only six and seven years old. I often had to go to the ski hill on weekends, so my time with Johnny was limited. It was hard to do things with our other children if Johnny couldn't participate. Consequently, Bryan, Bruce, and Beverly got neglected. I did take Bryan hunting with me some, usually just behind the ranger station.

Carl Marsh, the ranger, was a character. One day, I was at my desk in the back room of the office when a young man from Malmstrom Air Force Base came in. He asked where he could go to practice snowshoeing. Carl said, "You want to practice snowshoeing?" The man nodded. "I'll tell you what you do. Go back to Great Falls and buy two cinder blocks. Strap them on your feet, wet your pants and start walking." I couldn't believe my ears. Carl couldn't imagine anyone wanting to snowshoe that didn't have to.

Another time Sylvia, Carl's wife, and another lady whose name I don't remember were in the ranger's home, which was larger than the office. They were lying on the floor with their sweat pants on, exercising. A tourist stopped to ask directions, and thinking the ranger's house was the district office, came to the large bay window, looked into the living room, and then knocked on the door. I don't know what he thought, but the ladies told him what he wanted to know.

Sylvia had been raised Southern Baptist. Carl Marsh arranged for the Cascade County Mobile Library to stop at the ranger station, which was five miles from Neihart, the nearest town. Carl asked us all to check out books each time the Mobile Library came by, so they would continue to come. Sylvia missed church and Christian fellowship. She began to read spiritual books and made it known she wanted to go to church. Carl got in touch with a Methodist minister in Great Falls, who agreed to come to Monarch, a very small town north of the ranger station. There was an old, abandoned, white frame church in Monarch, and we arranged to use it. The pastor would come and hold services every other Sunday at two in the afternoon. On alternate weeks, he held a Bible study at the ranger's home. This continued until Carl was transferred, and then the Bible studies stopped.

In the fall of 1965, Bryan started first grade in Neihart. Sylvia had to drive him to school and pick him up in the afternoon, as there was no bus service. One winter, it was very cold at the ranger station. Sylvia bundled up the kids, put them in the car and headed to the school. About halfway there, she ran into a temperature inversion. The temperature went from below zero to above freezing, and immediately, the windows fogged so she couldn't see. That highway is narrow, goes through a narrow canyon and has lots of narrow curves. She stopped the car to wipe the windshield. Fortunately, there was no one behind her and she got to the school safely. The incident scared her, but she gave the Lord the credit for taking care of her and the kids.

The winter of 1965-66 was very cold. It got down to 50 below zero one night. The ranger station got its water from a small creek, across the highway and up the side hill, about 1/4 mile from the station. We had a water purification system that put chlorine into the water automatically. Carl was afraid the system would freeze, so he called and asked me to snowshoe with him up to the shed that housed the purification system. I remember I had to put a scarf over my nose to breathe through. Of course, everything was OK with the water. The shed was heated with an electric heater.

Carl transferred in January 1966 and was replaced by John Hook. John and his wife became good friends, and my duties continued as before. We continued to bring Johnny home on weekends.

During the summer of 1965 or '66, Sylvia took the kids to Alabama on the train. I had to work, so I stayed home. One day while she was gone, she phoned from Alabama. The ranger station had an old crank telephone in the office. The other residents had the same type of phones for inter-station communications only, and the only outside line was the one in the office. Our ring was one long and one short, and our number was Neihart 1. When Sylvia told the Alabama operator she wanted to place a long distance call to Neihart number 1, the operator told her there was no such number. Sylvia assured her that it was a toll call out of Great Falls, Montana. The operator checked with the Great Falls switchboard, and the call was completed. When I answered the phone, the Alabama operator asked if she could talk to me for a minute, and that she wouldn't charge for her time. I said OK, and she asked me to describe where I lived. Were there Indians around? What was it like? She finally thanked me and let me talk to my wife.

One weekend, I was the only one at the station when a carload of girls drove into our driveway, very excited. They said their parents owned a summer home (cabin) up a side road north of Neihart. They said the lights were on and it appeared someone was in the cabin. They asked me to get a gun and come see about it. I called the Deputy Sheriff in Neihart, Bun Stark. Bun said, "I'll meet you there." The only pistol I had was a .22 caliber revolver. I stuck the gun in my belt, to Sylvia's consternation, and drove up the canyon. Bun was waiting for me at the turnoff to the summer homes. When we got to the cabin, we could see that the light was on and the glass in the back door had been broken out. We approached the building with care and looked in the window. The burners on the electric stove were standing on end, and one was red hot. Flour, soot and other debris were scattered all over the stove and floor.

We determined that the intruder had been a bear. We checked the other cabins in the area and learned a couple of others had been broken into as well. I told Bun I wasn't comfortable meeting a bear with just a small caliber pistol, and he agreed. We reported the incident to the Fish and Game Department, and they trapped and moved a sow bear and two cubs from the area.

During our second year at Belt Creek Ranger Station, the Assistant Ranger, Jim Fishburn, married the Forest Supervisor's secretary. Jim had been living in the bunk house. To make room for his new wife, we got a mobile home and attached it to the bunk house. This was done while they were on their honeymoon. We decided to have a chivaree for the couple when they returned to the district, and Sylvia really got into it. We put saran wrap over the toilet, just under the seat. Someone tied bells to the bed springs. Sylvia put scotch tape over the faucets in the bathroom, so when you turned on the faucet, it squirted water in your face. Of course, the bed was short-sheeted. We had quite a party to welcome the married couple home.

John Hook, Jim Fishburn and I started to attend Toastmasters at Johnny's Bar in Belt, Montana. This was a great learning experience and a good social break for us. The group was made up of Belt schoolteachers, ranchers from the area and others. A State Representative and a Lieutenant Governor came out of our group. While we were eating, we had something called "table topics." The Table Topics Leader would go around the table and assign each of us a two-minute topic to do an extemporaneous speech on. One of our rancher members, an Angus cattle breeder, ordered a fellow who raised Hereford cattle to talk about why Angus was a better cattle breed. The only thing he could think of to talk about was sunburn. In the winter, when the sun reflects off the snow, cattle with light-colored bellies get sunburn, and when their udders are sunburned and sore, the mother cows often won't let their calves nurse. This, of course, doesn't occur with black Angus cattle. I had never known about the problems cattle ranchers face in Montana. On the night when it was my time to be "Toastmaster," the rancher who had talked about sunburn gave a formal speech. I introduced him as the man with the sunburned udders. This got a laugh, but the evaluator raked me over the coals for not putting my speaker at ease. He kept laughing at my remark during his speech, though. We didn't always follow the rules, but we had a lot of fun. I stayed with the group for about five years, even after I had moved to another ranger district.

CHAPTER 4
STANFORD MONTANA

In June 1967, I was transferred to the Judith Ranger District, headquartered in Stanford, Montana. I was still on the Lewis and Clark National Forest. Johnny came home for the summer. He entered fourth grade in the fall, and on weekends he would ride the Greyhound bus from Great Falls to Stanford. The School for the Blind would see him safely to the bus, and we would meet him when he arrived home. The trip was direct, with two stops in route. Johnny did fine, and the drivers got to know him.

At Stanford, my job was switched from timber management to range, special uses and recreation. I worked with John Inman the first year, and then Terry Johnson took his place. Terry's wife, Sue, was an ardent Christian. She and Sylvia soon became close friends, and Sylvia and the kids spent a lot of time with her. The summer of 1968, Johnny prayed with Sue and his mother to receive Jesus Christ as his personal savior. This was a life-changing experience for Johnny and would serve him well in the future. The women also spent a lot of time praying for me.

Doc Cornell was the District Ranger. We had been on the Donner Ridge fire together and gotten to know each other. Doc was an excellent horseman. He had raised horses, and they were his hobby. He decided I needed a horse for my range work, so he bought a big palomino horse from a sheepherder. He was a big, strong, fine-looking animal, but he was "cold backed" and tended to buck when you got on. We kept him at the Judith River guard station. I only rode him once. The District Ranger and range staff from Great Falls and I were going to ride into the west fork of the Judith River, and the trail started up a steep slope from the guard station. I led the horse to the foot of the slope before I mounted. He snorted and laid his ears back, and I kicked him and made him go straight up the hill. If he had bucked there, we would have both been hurt. By the time I got him to the top of the hill, he had settled down. The horse was a pleasure to ride, but frankly, I was afraid of him. Later, I was at a meeting with Gerald Hughes, one of our permit holders. He employed the sheepherder that we had bought the horse from. I told him about the horse, and he said, "Be careful of that horse, John. He's hurt lots of guys. They didn't break him until he was six years old." I told Doc what Gerald had said, and he sold the horse back to the herder.

Doc then bought a Missouri Foxtrotter for me to use. He was one of the best horses I ever rode. The Foxtrotter could walk eight miles per hour, and he outwalked any of the ranchers' horses I rode with. I also was assigned another palomino, since Doc didn't want me to ride the same horse two days in a row.

Another family we became acquainted with was Warren and Jenny Abrams. They ran the dry cleaners in Stanford and were devout Christians. Sylvia started to go to the Abrams's home every week for Bible study, in addition to spending a great deal of time with Sue Johnson. Christian literature began to appear around the house, and I would find Christian articles opened strategically in the bathroom, where I couldn't miss them. I began to complain. "What if someone came to our home and saw all that stuff scattered around? What would they think?" Sylvia just quietly picked up the papers and put them away.

We attended the Presbyterian Church in Stanford. I was asked to be an elder, and my ego was flattered, so I accepted. About that time, Warren asked if I would take him hunting . I said "sure," and that fall, we spent quite a bit of time together. He talked to me about the Lord and my faith, which was pretty shallow. I had been raised going to church and had been baptized when I was twelve, but I didn't really have a close relationship with the Lord. Warren asked if I had ever read in the Bible what it said about the conditions for being an elder. I hadn't looked at the Bible much, and I told Warren as much. He showed me the scriptures in Titus and Timothy. I sort of felt convicted, but I figured the rest of the elders in the church probably hadn't read those passages either.

In 1969, my father was serving his second term in the State Legislature in Helena and my mother was in a wheelchair, suffering from rheumatoid arthritis. In January, she caught the "Hong Kong" flu, which turned into pneumonia. She passed away in the Helena hospital at the age of 59. Dad was devastated. Just before she passed, he called me and said, "We're losing your mother." I left for Helena immediately. The roads were snow-packed and icy, and the going was slow. By the time I reached Helena, she was gone. I stayed to support Dad, and my brothers also came. We had the funeral in Bozeman, and Sylvia came with the kids. I don't remember, but I must have gone to Stanford to get the family, as we only had one car and an old pickup.

Bruce and Beverly both started first grade while we were in Stanford. Bryan and Bruce played little league baseball. Bryan was becoming a pretty good pitcher. Johnny continued to do very well in the School for the Blind and ride the bus home on weekends. In January 1970, his sixth-grade year, Johnny was mainstreamed into the public school in Great Falls, as part of an experiment to see how blind students did in a public school setting. The experiment worked well for John. In the fall of 1970, they were planning to place him in the public school in Stanford. His books were either translated into Braille or recorded on tape. However, before the transition could be made, I was transferred to the Gallatin Ranger District, Gallatin National Forest, twenty-five miles from Bozeman, Montana, in the Gallatin Canyon. This turned out even better for Johnny, except that the School for the Blind had to re-do his books to conform to the Bozeman Junior High School.

Bruce had a problem with nightmares. They had started when he was about two, when we were still at Belt Creek. He would wake us up screaming. We would go to his room and try to wake him, but he would sit up and continue to dream and holler. After we got to Stanford and he was a little older, his mother taught him to pray when he had a bad dream. We also would go in and pray with him. The nightmares went away.

CHAPTER 5
BOZEMAN

The summer of 1970 was a bad fire year on the Lewis and Clark National Forest. The District Ranger, Doc Cornell, retired and I was Acting Ranger for a time. In August, Howard Challenor reported for duty. He had not been on the district but a short time when we had a bad lightning storm. The next morning, since I knew the district, we had the patrol plane stop and take me on board to look for lightning fires. We found several, but before we landed, we were ordered to White Sulphur Springs, to a fire that was growing rapidly to project size. I was assigned to the fire as a Sector Boss. Howard brought my things and was also assigned as a scout. He got trapped in a blow up while scouting the fire, and he saved himself by lying in a creek and putting his face in a hole on the side of the creek bank. However, he suffered severe burns. I was sent back to the district and continued as Acting Ranger while Howard recuperated in the hospital.

In September 1970, I was offered a promotion and new position on the Gallatin Ranger District, headquartered twenty-five miles south of Bozeman in the Gallatin Canyon. My dad helped us find a home in Bozeman. Until then, we had either lived in Government housing or rented. The four-bedroom, split-level house at 1501 South Black was our home for the next ten years.

One decision that I still feel bad about was my decision to euthanize our dog, Tammy. She was a very hyper dog, used to running loose, and very possessive of our family. I didn't know anyone that I could give her to. We were going to live in the city of Bozeman, which had strict leash laws. To take the dog with us, I thought, was out of the question. I was sure that if we penned her up she would bark and be a nuisance. We talked it over, and neither Sylvia or any of the kids said anything, so I took the dog to a vet and he put her to sleep. It turned out that the reason my kids didn't say anything was they were speechless. The kids had trouble forgiving me for it and would bring it up at times, saying, "You killed our dog." I'm not sure what I would have done differently, but if I had to do it over, I would have thought of another alternative.

Johnny started seventh grade at Bozeman Junior High. The rest of the kids also attended Bozeman schools. Bryan was in sixth grade, Bruce was in fourth and Bev in second grade. They had to enter the schools after the year had already started, which was hard on them.

We attended Grand Avenue Christian Church, the church I had grown up in. Sylvia and I wanted the kids to go to Sunday school, so we attended an adult class taught by Roger Wilson, a professor at Montana State University. Roger challenged us to try an experiment by doing a program called "Ten Brave Christians" or "A Life That Really Matters." The challenge was to see if living a disciplined Christian life for one month would make a difference. There were exactly five couples, including Sylvia and me, who agreed to the challenge. It was early

January, 1971. We were to get up at 5:30 a.m. and spend ten minutes reading an assigned scripture verse and writing in a journal what it meant to us, spend ten minutes praying about an unselfish act we could do that day, and ten minutes writing what we wanted in life. The latter was to be only one or two sentences each day. We were to get together with the other participants one night each week, to share, pray together and compare notes.

The night before the experiment was to start, I set the alarm for 5:30, but the thought came to me that I might just shut off the alarm and go back to sleep. At 5:28 the next morning, I got a charley horse in my left leg that brought me out of bed, rubbing a knot in my calf. About that time, the alarm went off, and I figured God wanted me to work the program and that He had a sense of humor. I went into the living room and opened the lesson book. As I thought about what good deed I could do, I remembered an incident that had occurred a month after I had come to Bozeman.

There was a veteran of World War II who had a brain injury, but he owned a cabin (summer home) on Forest Service land under a special use permit. I had inspected the cabin that fall, and it was a mess. The owner had started several repair projects but hadn't finished any of them. Bags of cement under the porch had gotten wet and hardened. There were poles and lumber scattered around the building, and several other problems. I had called on the man to talk about getting his cabin into compliance with Forest Service regulations. It turned out that he was taking care of his older, invalid mother, and he had health issues himself. He just hadn't been able to spend much time at the summer home. I had suggested that there were several people interested in having a cabin in the forest, and that maybe he could sell it.

Because of his mental condition, this caused him a great deal of stress. I also had followed up our visit with a letter on official stationary, reiterating what we had talked about. This probably contributed to his being admitted to the Veteran's Hospital in Sheridan, Wyoming. I had received a phone call from his pastor, who told me of the man being in the hospital. The pastor told me that one of the things bothering the veteran was my letter. He asked if some of the men in his church could go up and clean the area around the cabin, and I told him, "Of course, and I will go with you, but there is snow on the ground now. It would be better to wait until spring."

I had all but forgotten the incident, but on the morning of the great experiment, the event came back to my memory and I couldn't get it out of my mind. I thought, "Maybe I could shovel his walks or something." Later that morning, I called the man's pastor and learned he had just returned from the hospital, that his mother was at his sister's in Helena and he was home alone. The pastor suggested I call the man and visit with him. As soon as I hung up, I made the phone call. When I told him everything was going to be taken care of by his church, I could hear the tension go out of his voice. We had a short but cordial conversation.

A couple of days later, I had to go up the Canyon on Forest Service business. I got into a pickup at the ranger station and started up the highway. I had gone a few miles when I noticed that the gas gauge read empty. There is a standing rule in the Forest Service that you must always return vehicles with a full tank, as you never know when there will be a rescue or other emergency. We had a gas pump at the station, so there had been no excuse for not fueling the vehicle. Anyway, I said a prayer and asked the Lord to let me get to Karst Camp, where there was gas available. When I pulled into Karst, the fuel-gauge needle wasn't even quivering. I filled up, and the tank took 15.2 gallons. When I looked in the owner's manual, it said the fuel capacity was 15 gallons. My prayer had been answered, and then some.

As a result of these incidents, the next morning I gave my life to Jesus Christ. I told Him in prayer that He could have my life, my money, my family, my job, etc., and I meant it. I had a strange feeling of complete lack of control for a moment, and then a warm feeling of peace came over me. I thought I might be called to go to Africa or something, but that didn't happen. What did happen was a complete paradigm change. I was excited, and from then on I wanted to be as close to the Lord as I could get.

Sylvia was excited also. Church took on new meaning. The "Ten Brave Christians" experiment had ended, but we continued to meet for prayer and Bible study. One couple, Grant and Lillian Cole, left the group. Grant had been our pastor, but he took a new church in Grant's Pass, Oregon. Bruce and Inez Bobb joined us, and Bruce became our leader. One of the things we did at the Bible study was exchange books. I kept reading about the "Baptism of the Holy Spirit" in books that I took home. There was a book by an Episcopal priest, another by a Southern Baptist, and one by a Christian Church pastor, all talking about this experience of "speaking in tongues." As I read their stories, I began to wonder if Sylvia hadn't had that experience. She'd never told me about it, but I suspected she was "spirit filled." I decided that I wanted to have that gift, as well. I asked Sylvia if she spoke in tongues, and she replied that she did. When I asked her why she hadn't told me, she said, "You weren't ready." She was right about that, but I was ready now. I asked her to pray with me, which she did, but nothing happened.

I was determined, however, and I phoned the Assembly of God pastor, John Weaver. I told him I wanted to receive the Baptism of the Holy Spirit and asked for an appointment with him. John was silent for a moment. "Are you there?" I asked. He acknowledged that he was, and told me he could see me that morning, Saturday, but to give him thirty minutes. I thought, "Boy, this is service." I had expected an appointment in a week or two.

When I got to the church, John called me into his office and asked me questions to be sure I had a relationship with Jesus. He had phoned his assistant, Joe Barnet, and one of his church elders, whom I will call "Don." We went to a room in the back of the church that had several old pews in it. They called it their "prayer room." The men had me kneel down at one of the pews, and they laid their hands on me and began to pray. I did not know any of these men at the time, and I was not real comfortable. They started to pray in tongues, and I felt like I was going to cry. I had been taught from childhood that men don't cry, so I fought the feeling, but as I was struggling, John began to weep as he was praying for me. I lost it! I cried for the first time in thirty years. I washed the bench with my tears. It was embarrassing, and I wanted to leave. I stood up, and the pastor gave me a hug. That bothered me also, as I was not used to being hugged by a man; that was what women did. John looked me in the eye and said, "You've asked and you have received, now just believe and the prayer language will come." I don't remember that those were his exact words, but they are close.

I felt embarrassed and stupid as I drove home. I figured I had really made a fool of myself. The next morning was Sunday, and I told Sylvia I was not going to church. She said nothing, but loaded the kids in the car and left. I sat in my recliner and prayed. Actually, I talked out loud to the Lord. I asked Him what this was all about. What more did I need to do to find favor with him? I knew I was a sinner, but the Bible says we can be forgiven of our sins. I racked my brain for something I had done that I hadn't asked forgiveness for. I continued to talk to the Lord out loud, and suddenly, I began to speak in what sounded like a foreign language, only I didn't know what I was saying. I could speed up the speech or slow it down, start or stop it, but I had no control of what was coming out of my mouth. I had a feeling of ecstasy that I can't explain. It was wonderful!

After a few moments of basking in the presence of the Holy Spirit, I looked at my watch. "I can still get to Sunday school," I thought. Our old Volkswagon was outside, so I took it to the church. When I walked into the class, the pastor's wife looked at me and said, "John has had an experience." I don't know what she saw, but she was sure right.

Shortly after that, I received a phone call from Ralph Porter, who identified himself as president of "The Full Gospel Business Men's Fellowship" in Bozeman. He invited me to come to the Baxter Hotel the next Saturday and share my testimony. I had never heard of the organization and I wondered how they knew about me, but I agreed. I soon joined the fellowship, and at the next election of officers, I was elected treasurer.

My enthusiasm got me elected to the elder board of the Grand Avenue Christian Church. The pastor didn't agree with the theology of what I claimed happened to me, but he couldn't doubt my enthusiasm.

The Baptism of the Holy Spirit was then and still is quite controversial. At the time I received my gift, the experience was relatively popular, and the charismatic movement had spread to most of the mainline churches, both Catholic and Protestant. The church I attended was no exception. We had a young college student, John Brownell, working with the youth in the church. One night when we were having a potluck supper, John Brownell took five or six high school students to one of the Sunday school rooms and talked to them about speaking in tongues. Our pastor, who was quite liberal, found out what was going on. He found me and told me that John was having a séance upstairs, and he was going up to throw him out of the church. I went with him. We walked in, and before we got past the greetings, I said, "Let's pray." I pled the blood of Jesus over the room and everyone in it, and I came against Satan and bound him in the name of Jesus.

I don't think the pastor had ever heard a prayer like that, certainly not from me, and for a moment, he was speechless. I told John Brownell and the kids that what they were doing was probably not appropriate for our church, but I invited them to meet in our home, which they did.

John and a couple of college girls started a Bible study for high school kids in our home. Some nights, there would be forty kids sitting in chairs and on couches and on the floor of our living room. Sylvia served cookies and lemonade, and we watched and listened. One night, one of the girls took me aside and told me of a dream or vision she had experienced. She said, "The Lord told me to tell you." I was skeptical but listened to her story. She said that the Lord was going to do a great thing in Bozeman: There was to be a "Conference on the Holy Spirit," and people would be filled with the Spirit from several churches and denominations. I don't recall the exact words, but that was the gist.

I put the incident out of my mind, but the next Saturday morning, we had a staff meeting of the Full Gospel Business Men, and Don, one of the men who had prayed with me at the Assembly of God Church, told us he had a vision from the Lord. As he told the story, I realized it was very similar to the one the girl related to me at our home. We were excited, and that was the beginning of several conventions of the Full Gospel Business Men in Bozeman—across Montana, for that matter. As club treasurer, I knew our bank balance was around $80. On faith, we contacted five speakers and began to plan a big "Conference on the Holy Spirit." We had two Christian psychologists, one a Roman Catholic. We had a Spirit-filled Baptist, a Lutheran, and a Pentecostal, all from out of town. Our expenses were around $4000, as I remember. Don did not want to take an offering. He said, "The Lord will provide." We just had a bucket on a table in the foyer of the auditorium. When the conference was over, we met all expenses and our bank balance was again $80.

The conference was fantastic. One night, we had 55 people from many different churches come forward to receive the Holy Spirit. The speaker motioned to me and had me pray with a man who turned out to be the President of the Knights of Columbus, Ed Halvorson. The night Ed came forward, I had only been a serious Christian for less than a year and had never prayed for anyone to receive the Baptism of the Holy Spirit. We prayed, and the Lord honored our prayer. Ed spoke in tongues and together, we praised the Lord and celebrated. Then Ed asked me my name. I replied, "Why do you want to know?" He said, "I want to remember who gave me this gift." I said, "It's spelled J-e-s-u-s." I was more than a little nervous. Then Ed said, "What am I going to tell my friends?" "About what?" I replied. "That I have quit drinking and smoking," Ed told me. I commented, "Have you?" "Oh, I could never do that again, after what the Lord has done for me," Ed answered.

It was a great night. A year later, I was elected president of the Full Gospel Business Men, and Ed became vice president and worship leader. Ed was an accomplished musician and guitar player. We bonded, and our friendship grew. We are still close friends today.

I continued to get up early and spend time in prayer and Bible reading. I had a long list of people I was praying for. One morning as I was praying, when I got to Sylvia's cousin and her husband, Mildred and John Russ, I felt a warm rush come over me. I know it was the Holy Spirit; it felt wonderful, and I didn't want it to go away. I was prone on the living room floor and for a few moments I just lay there, basking in the presence of the Holy Spirit. I started to continue with my prayer list, and the feeling went away.

I went back and started praying again for John and Mildred, and the feeling came back. Mildred's husband John had been seriously wounded in Korea when he was with the Marines. He still had shrapnel in his leg. He had not been able to work for a while and then got a job working for the City of Camden, Arkansas water plant. One day, several bags of chlorine had fallen on him, injuring his back and putting him in a wheelchair. His wife, Mildred, had called for prayer. He was in constant pain and was paralyzed from the waist down.

I went into the bedroom and told Sylvia I was going to call her cousin. It turned out that John had been miraculously healed. He had been in severe pain, and the doctors had given him pain medicine, but it was no longer working, so they were contemplating surgery to sever the nerves in John's back to relieve the pain. This would have left him paralyzed for life. John had been reading a book by Charles Capps, a Pentecostal evangelist, on faith healing. He prayed, and the Lord healed him. When I talked to him, he was on fire for the Lord and had started reading his Bible. We were excited for John and also for the way the Lord chose to let us know about it.

We were anxious to visit John and Mildred, so the next summer, we drove south with the kids for a visit. We were headed for Alabama, but wanted to stop off in Camden to hear firsthand about John Russ's experience. The Russes had a large home, and we were all able to stay with them. We spent the entire visit talking about the Lord. One afternoon, Beverly and I went for a walk to get some air. We planned to just walk around the neighborhood. As we walked past one house, a dog came off a porch and came after us, barking. The hair on his back was standing up. I had never done this before, but I pointed my finger at the dog and said out loud, "In the name of Jesus, be still!" At once, the dog sat down and was quiet. As we walked, we had the same experience two more times. I have to admit, I was more than a little surprised. Beverly was impressed. When we returned to Montana, she had a similar incident walking home from school. There was an old railroad bed behind our house that used to be a spur line for the Milwaukee Railroad. The kids used to walk to and from school on the old right of way, as it was a short cut. One day as Beverly was coming home with one of her friends, two Doberman Pinschers came after them. Bev remembered our experience in Camden and commanded the dogs to be still in the name of Jesus. The dogs sat down immediately, impressing Bev's friend.

In 1972, Bryan began to visit a hobby store in downtown Bozeman, and he got the notion he wanted a fish tank for tropical fish. We got it for him, and he began to spend his allowance on fish. He and his friend Ron McMichael also got some minnows, which turned out to be whitefish, and put them in the tank. The next morning, they had jumped out. We found them on the floor. Next, he got interested in an "N" gauge model railroad. For his birthday, we bought him a starter kit. He began to use his allowance to buy cars, track and model houses, and he took over the ping-pong table in the recreation room. He and his friends built a large layout, with a mountain, train tunnel, scale model houses and other items they created. He spent a lot of time in our basement with his friends.

Bruce was getting good on his guitar, but he still played rock music with his friend, Charlie Reed. I recognized the talent but didn't appreciate the music, which sounded like so much noise to me. They also listened to tapes of rock music stars of the time.

One day some friends of ours, Don and Becky Berglund, told us about a new pastor who had come to town. He was holding a Bible study at a home on the north side of town, and Don said we should come and check it out. We went to the study and met Chris and Judy Blackmore. He had been with Campus Crusade For Christ at both Montana State University and the University of Montana and was starting a church, affiliated with "The Evangelical Church of North America." Sylvia and I were intrigued with the way he taught the Bible, and we began attending on a regular basis. At one meeting, Chris told us of an evangelist named Bill Gothard, who was going to be speaking in Portland, Oregon. He said he would like to attend and wanted to know if any of us were interested in going. We decided to go, and six of us—Chris and Judy, Don and Becky and Sylvia and I—attended the event together. We drove my Ford station wagon straight through to Portland. Chris had arranged for us to stay at George Fox College in one of the married student houses. I remember it was old and kind of rundown, but it served the purpose.

The event was held at a big coliseum. About 20,000 people from all over the Northwest came in chartered busses and filled the building. The overflow was in a separate room with closed circuit TV. Bill Gothard was on stage, and there were two big screens on either side of him, where he was televised as well. He held us spellbound for hours. I remember he made the statement that if we were in a church where we couldn't submit to our pastor as our spiritual elder, we should find another place to worship.

This, I felt, was my situation. I knew at that moment that I needed to find a different church. Before we left, we all received lapel pins with the initials PBPGINFWMY. This translates: Please Be Patient, God Is Not Finished With Me Yet.

The ride home was the same as the trip over. We traveled all the way to Bozeman without stopping, except for gas. We would change drivers as necessary and sleep the best we could with our head on someone's shoulder or on a cold window.

The next Sunday, I told the pastor of the Christian Church I was leaving and wanted to meet with the elders. I was an elder and vice chairman of the Church board. I liked the pastor, but his theology was very liberal. He didn't believe in the virgin birth or the bodily resurrection of Christ, and he didn't believe in the existence of Satan, among other things. I had spent many hours with him, talking about these things to no avail and to my considerable frustration. Once when I was in his office and he was preparing his sermon, I was witnessing to him when he threw me a hymnal and told me to pick out a song for the communion service. I opened the book, and it fell open to the old hymn, "There's Power In The Blood." When I suggested that one, he said, "Pick something else. We can't have people getting sick by singing about blood just before we take communion."

At the elders meeting, I announced why I was leaving. They gave me their blessing and were quite supportive. Later, I had a chance to meet with a couple of them and share in more detail. On reflection, I'm not proud of the way I did that, but I reasoned that since I was an elder and on the Board, I owed it to the church to tell them why I was leaving. Shortly after that meeting, several others left the church as well. That pastor soon left for another church. I have prayed for him often, and honestly, I feel some guilt for the way I handled my resignation. At least, everyone heard it from me and there was no reason to speculate or gossip.

We became members of the Bozeman Evangelical Church of North America. We first met at the old Elk's Country Club, near the cemetery. Later, we moved into the Seventh Day Adventist Church. They used it on Saturdays, and we rented it on Sundays. We began to grow under the Bible teaching of Chris Blackmore. Sylvia even went through a deliverance. She had been raised Southern Baptist, and the teaching at our old church conflicted with the way she had been raised. Chris told her to read the Word of God and the confusion would go away. He was right, and that is exactly what happened.

Don and Becky Berglund hosted a Bible study in their home, which we attended for several years, until we started one of our own.

CHAPTER 6
GALLATIN RANGER DISTRICT

I continued to work with the Forest Service as the Assistant Ranger for range, recreation, and special uses, commuting twenty-five miles from my home in Bozeman to Squaw Creek Ranger Station. The District Ranger was Bob Cron, an excellent supervisor and hard worker. We worked together for several years.

I had grown up in Bozeman and attended school there, and when I was growing up, my grandmother had a summer home in the Gallatin Canyon at Goose Creek, a small drainage between Karst Camp and what is now Big Sky. Consequently, I had spent a lot of time in the Canyon before I was stationed there, and my family knew many of the long-time residents. When I discovered that an old family friend, Roy Walton, was building a bridge across the Gallatin River, I had a problem. Any disturbance of the Gallatin River, a navigable stream by classification (because they used to float railroad ties down the river to Central Park), required permits from the Army Corps of Engineers, Montana Fish, Wildlife and Parks and the Forest Service. Roy had none of these, but he had a mining claim on the east side of the river, as well as a cabin and land, which he had subdivided and sold to three other owners. The latter had also built cabins.

I was driving down the canyon one day and noticed a bulldozer in the river. I stopped to find out what was going on. The dozer operator told me to talk to Roy, as he had hired them. I made an appointment to talk with Mr. Walton that afternoon. When I knocked on his door, he recognized me and invited me in. He started talking right away, asking about my dad. When I told him he was in Arizona, he started telling me a story about taking two millionaires pig hunting in Arizona. It was about thirty minutes before I could get a word in, to tell him why I was there. He said, "I've always tried to get along with you government boys. You fix up the papers, and I'll sign 'em." I talked to the Supervisor's Office, and since Roy had the legal right of ingress and egress to his property, and he was replacing an existing bridge, we worked with him. He was in his eighties and had lived in the county most of his life. He had purchased two railroad flatcars, planned to build two new abutments and one central piling, and weld the two flatcars together for his bridge. We issued him the necessary permits for construction, but before we issued the final special use permit, the Forest Engineers had to inspect the bridge for soundness and quality of construction.

The day of the inspection in August, I met Roy, accompanied by one of our engineers, Dutch Wheaton. While Dutch, a very competent engineer, climbed over the side of the bridge to inspect the welds and make notes, I stood on the bridge talking to Roy. He said, "You see that telephone line going across the river?" I nodded. "Well, there ain't no phones on the east side of the river. I just strung that line to keep me in fishing tackle. When I need something, I just shoot down what I need with my pistol and catch it in a net." Indeed, there was an old fishing leader with a hook and spinner hanging from what looked like a single phone line. Roy watched Dutch do his job for a few minutes, then asked, "You build very many bridges in your day? I've built lots of them in my day." The bridge passed inspection, and because it was pretty narrow, we insisted that a locked gate be placed on the bridge to keep the general public from using it. This suited Roy fine. Times have changed. This would not work in today's world.

Big Sky was being developed in the West Fork of the Gallatin River. Chet Huntley, the famous newscaster, was a stockholder in the Big Sky Corporation, and since he had retired from broadcasting, he was promoting the new resort. Part of the development was on National Forest land, so we were involved with permits and avalanche control on the ski area. Later, the area was sold to Boyne Mountain Corporation. The activity generated a good deal of work for the Forest Service.

Law enforcement was just one of the problems we worked with. The new construction attracted all sorts of characters to work in the area. One summer, several young men decided to camp in the woods above Big Sky Meadow Village. The camp took on the look of a settlement. They were making a big mess, and our regulations limited recreational camping to fourteen days. We did not allow people to set up permanent residence. They had no place to dispose of their garbage, and of course, there were no sanitary facilities. This created a strong potential for fire as the summer progressed. I had tried to catch up with the men and had left notes on their cars, with no results. I talked to the County Attorney about the problem, and he arranged for two Sheriff's deputies to accompany me to the campsite. We left early the next morning to arrive at the camp before the men left for work. When we arrived at the campsite, there were two cars present, one without a license. The men were asleep in their tent.

We woke the sleepers and ordered them out of the tent. They slowly emerged, rubbing their eyes and squinting at the morning sun. They had been smoking marijuana. Their eyes were dilated, and they talked with little voice inflection or show of emotion. "Hey man, what's up?" one of the young men remarked. We told them they had to clean up the area and that they couldn't camp there. I issued them citations for littering and illegal camping. They looked at the papers I handed them and said, "Crazy, man." One of the deputies, a big man named Hank Feddes, asked who owned the Volkswagen with no license plates. One of the young men acknowledged it was his car. "Let me see your registration," Hank said. "Man, I don't have any, I just bought the car." "Then show me your bill of sale," Hank said. "Hey, I don't know where it is," said the young man. Hank told him, "I'm not going to mess around with you, young man. Show me the bill of sale or a registration, or I'm taking you in for car theft." The man reached for his billfold and produced a paper, which the Deputy examined and gave back. We inspected the surrounding area, finding several places where they had relieved themselves and left toilet paper and strewn garbage. We warned the men to clean up the place, and we left.

I was disappointed, because I had been looking for one particular man who had been giving us trouble all summer. He was the leader of the group, but he hadn't been there. That afternoon, the fellow I was looking for stormed into our office at Squaw Creek. Besides the secretary, the only other person in the office was Nick Finzer, the Timber Management Assistant. The intruder started threatening me, and while he talked, I wrote him a citation. Nick came in and stood by my desk while I wrote the violation notice. Nick had been a Green Beret in Vietnam, and I was grateful for his backup.

Besides law enforcement, my work consisted of managing the range, wildlife, recreation, wilderness, and land uses of all kinds, including administering special use permits for summer homes, outfitting and guiding, and the Big Sky development in the West Fork of the Gallatin. In addition, I attended many planning, training, and budget meetings. Ranger Cron was a pleasure to work with, and we worked well together.

CHAPTER 7
JOHNNY AND SCHOOL

When Sylvia and I got married, she had completed two years of a three-year study to become a registered nurse. We got married and moved clear across the country, so she never finished her RN training. However, Bozeman had a vocational training program at that time, and one of the courses offered was training to be a Licensed Practical Nurse, LPN. Sylvia wanted to enroll, but we didn't have the money. Sylvia's friend Francis Carter, who was an RN, offered to pay the registration fee. We didn't want her to, and my pride said we should save up for the next time the course was offered. However, Francis insisted, so we took the money and Sylvia enrolled. Since she already had two years of nurse training, and because she studied and worked hard, she finished second in her class. We will always be indebted to Francis for her kindness.

Johnny always rode the bus to school. The other kids did too, when they got into junior high and high school. That is, they rode the bus if there was no other alternative. Johnny used his mobility training and walked with a white cane. Originally, he had to walk about two blocks to South Willson to catch the school bus. Our neighbor, Ella Mae Terpstra, drove a school bus, and one day she saw Johnny, who was a little late, try to run to the bus stop and fall. He wasn't hurt, but Ella Mae complained on Johnny's behalf. Karst Stage altered the bus route, and from then on, John's bus stopped at our front door.

Johnny was interested in music. He loved to sing and began making up songs about the Lord. We decided to get him guitar lessons. Steve Carlson ran a music store in the Bozeman Hotel, called "The Back Porch Picking Parlor." He was an expert on the guitar and banjo, and he went to our church, so we asked him to teach Johnny. We tried to get Bruce lessons, too. John caught on and learned the instrument right away. Bruce was slower and would not do what Steve wanted him to, so we dropped his lessons but kept on with Johnny. Bruce ended up teaching himself and would practice in his room for hours. He got quite good on the guitar, but he mostly played rock music.

Johnny would make up ballad-style songs, and he was good enough that he sang them for the church. He had a beautiful voice. He had a strange way of naming his songs, however: one was called, "The Shower Song," because he was taking a shower when it came to him. Another he called, "Grandma's Couch," for the same reason. He made up one song with his brother, Bruce, a praise song based on Psalm 150. Later, when we decided to have the songs copyrighted, our friend Ed Halverson wrote down the words and music to many of them so we could submit them to the Copyright Office.

Because of John's lack of sight, the junior high and later the high school set him up in his own office, where he kept his Braille books and audio tapes. When he was not in class, he would go to his office and study. When he was in high school, he wrote a poem, "A Student's Prayer" for an English class. District Judge W. W. Lessley received a copy, had it framed and placed it in his office. The poem was as follows:

Down an empty hall I walk,
Empty of people, empty of talk.
They dismissed us early today,
But that's all right; I need to pray.

I'd like to pray for that exam;
I stayed up so late, I had to cram.
On top of that, I'm almost spastic
From doing all that work in gymnastics.
I still haven't gotten over that fall
I took while running down the hall.
The test that's due today is going to be late.
I just can't seem to keep anything straight.
And yet, my notebook's a mess
and my math book is too;
I've still got lots of math to do.
Got English to do and history and speech,
That work is so hard to breech.

I see the people as class passing time comes,
Louder and louder are their hums.
Especially Lord, I'd like to pray
For these people I meet along the way;
The guy who trys his very best,
But just can't seem to pass that test,
For kids who make the honor roll
But feel so empty in their soul,
For those on clubs and those on teams,
For those with hopes and those with dreams

Who take a challenge or a dare,
And also for those who just don't care.
For broken family situations,
For those in special education,
And Lord, I want to pray so much
For principals, teachers, coaches, and such.
For those who are hits and those who are jocks,
Jesus freaks, and those who throw rocks,
For those who feel they have no friends
And–
Oh, Lord, this could go on without end.
Though all these people, Lord, you see
I pray for them and they pray for me.

It seems your name has become obscene,
I know there are others–very few,
Who come to know You as I do.
Lord, please bless them each today
As they pass along life's way.

The bell's ringing now, I have to go.
Go with me through the traffic flow
And help me, Lord, to love to share
To show them that you really care,
So you can help them to find out,
What life is really all about.
They'd all say that I'm a fool,
But Lord, I really pray for school.

Today, the public schools would not permit a student to write about the Lord and prayer. Johnny wrote this when he was about a junior in high school. At that time, there was quite a movement of students coming to the Lord at Bozeman High School

One of the Physical Education teachers taught Johnny gymnastics. He worked on the parallel bars and the rings, and he got good enough to put on a halftime show at one of the basketball games. Johnny also was on the speech team and won several trophies. He took second place in the state in Oral Interpretation. Johnny had his speech written in Braille. When he delivered his speech, he read the Braille by running his finger over the paper, which was on the speaker's podium. One of the judges, who didn't realize he was blind, marked him down for running his finger over the paper while he was speaking.

About this time, there was a new pastor at the Church of God who was trying to get a Christian school started. His name was Butch Goan, and we really liked him. We felt Johnny had a pretty good deal in the public school, and he only had one more year before graduating, but we were interested in placing the other kids at Butch's school. Butch had been in some kind of disfavor with his bishop, and he resigned from the Church of God but was immediately hired by the Assembly of God, who helped him get the school started in their church building. Bev, Bruce, and Bryan all attended, and Bryan was in the first graduating class.

Meanwhile, Johnny finished his senior year. He had made the National Honor Society as a junior, and he was asked to be class speaker at graduation. As I recall, there were about 300 students who graduated in 1976. Johnny wouldn't tell me what he was going to talk about, but he asked me to pray for him. Graduation was held in the fieldhouse at Montana State University. Sylvia and I attended with my father. Johnny's talk was on "Friends." He talked about the friends he had made among the students and teachers, naming several of them. Then he said, "There is one friend I wish you all knew, Jesus Christ."

The students all stood to give him a standing ovation, and the whole auditorium followed the students' lead. Some people sitting behind us in the balcony said, "I wonder whose son that is." Dad turned around and said, "That's my grandson." It was a proud day for all of us.

Our friend Karen Williamson, who lived a few doors down the street from us on south Black, took an interest in Johnny and did the paperwork for him to get an Elks Club scholarship. He also got a scholarship to a school run by the Lions Club in Little Rock, Arkansas. This school for blind students taught vocational education and had a college preparatory course, which Johnny enrolled in. The class taught the students to deal with various living skills and things they would need to deal with in college. We drove Johnny to Little Rock and got him settled in his dorm. Sylvia's cousin and her husband, John and Mildred Russ, lived 100 miles south, in Camden. They would come and get Johnny on weekends, which was a comfort to us.

When Johnny completed the school in Little Rock, we brought him home and he enrolled at the University of Montana, in Missoula. He wanted to take journalism, but the Dean of the Journalism School talked him out of it. He felt a career in journalism would be out of the question for a blind person. As a result, Johnny majored in English.

During our almost ten-year stay in Bozeman, from September 1970 to May 1980, we were active in the Evangelical Church, the Full Gospel Business Men's Fellowship, one or two Bible studies per week, and I was on the Board of Directors of the Carpenter's Workshop in West Yellowstone.

In 1978, the Bozeman chapter of the Full Gospel Business Men held a convention at the Montana State University Student Union Ballroom. Johnny was asked to sing several numbers that he had written. One of the people in attendance was Wayne Fisher, who owned and operated a recording studio in Cozad, Nebraska. After hearing Johnny, he approached me and told me Johnny's songs should be recorded. He offered us a deal. All we would have to pay for was his out of pocket costs; he would not charge us for his labor. He gave me his card and told me he could get additional musicians to back Johnny, if he made the recording.

Instead of responding right away, we took it to prayer. Even with Wayne donating his time, the recording would still cost about $2,000. I didn't have the money, but I put out a fleece. We prayed that if my dad would loan us the money, we would take it as a sign that we should go ahead with the deal. I approached my dad, and he didn't even hesitate. He wrote us a check.

John was at school in Missoula, so we began to make plans on the telephone. Johnny had a friend, Robert Merritt, who had played music with him in Missoula, and he wanted him to play bass guitar. I made the arrangements, and we set a date to go to Cozad for the recording. When the time came, John and Robert came to our house in Bozeman and spent the night. That evening, Robert was opening a jar of canned peaches and it broke, cutting his hand. I dressed the wound and thought we would have to cancel the recording, but Robert thought he would be OK

The next day, John, Robert and I left for Nebraska. Sylvia stayed behind with our other kids. Wayne and his wife Robbie lived in an old schoolhouse on the edge of a wheat field, about a mile north of Interstate 80. The studio was in the basement of the schoolhouse. It was ideal for a recording studio, as there was no railroad, no airplanes, no highway, just a gravel country road with only occasional traffic. It took part of two days to record ten songs. We stayed with Wayne and Robbie. When we finished, we returned home and waited for the records to arrive. They came in time for Christmas 1979.

My good friend Ed Halvorson made arrangements for a concert at the Willson Auditorium in Bozeman, featuring John and his music. He also invited another blind girl, D. D. Dunn, to sing at intermission. The concert was well attended, and we sold enough records to repay John's grandpa for the loan. We will always be indebted to Ed for his work with John.

1978-79 was the last year of high school at Christian Center. The school board had decided to drop the high school program and just continue kindergarten through eighth grade. Bruce was a senior, and Bev was a sophomore. We were shocked to learn that Bruce was using marijuana and skipping school. As a result, he didn't graduate. Bruce and Bev both enrolled in Bozeman Senior High in the fall of 1979. Bruce continued to skip school and finally dropped out. He later completed his GED. Bruce tells his own story in the next chapter.

CHAPTER 8
BRUCE

From the time I was two until six years old, I suffered strange nightmares. I would dream of swelling foreheads on members of my family, and of being attacked. My eyes would seem to get stuck on the corners of the room, where the walls and ceiling came together, and I would panic and scream. Mom would come to my room and try to comfort me, but I wouldn't snap out of it.

Mom talked to her friend Sue Johnson about this, and they both prayed and took authority over what they believed to be demons. Mom then told me I could pray to Jesus and ask Him to not let me have any more bad dreams. I did this, and the nightmares stopped.

I gave my life to the Lord and was baptized in the Holy Spirit when I was fourteen; however, I began to play and listen to rock music that was very dark. I also started to sneak out and smoke pot with strange kids that I met. I felt rejected and needed attention from others, especially my parents, but I didn't show it. I liked doing my own thing, and I didn't do well in school. I began to be jealous of my siblings, especially Johnny and my mother, and I became mad at God.

One day, I lost my wallet containing about forty dollars and my driver's license. I was not happy, to say the least. Mom was cooking in the kitchen when I told her about it. She prayed and then suddenly pointed her finger at me and said, "To prove to you that God is real, your wallet will be returned to you with the money and license, in the name of Jesus Christ, Amen." A short time later, the doorbell rang and Dad answered it. A young man we had never seen before was at the door with my wallet. He said, "I just couldn't take the money." I was downstairs in my room and heard the entire conversation. I was trembling.

I was supposed to graduate in the spring of 1979, but I had skipped so much school, and my grades were poor, that I was scheduled to go one more year. Since Christian Center dropped their high school program, I would have to enter Bozeman High. The summer of 1979, my dad helped me get into the Youth Conservation Corps. I was stationed at the Swan Lake Ranger Station, south of Glacier Park. That summer, I worked on trails, learned to build fences and other work as assigned.

I started school in the Fall, but started to cut classes again and eventually dropped out. Eventually, I got my G.E.D.

My dad felt I needed to do something with my life, so he got me into the Young Adult Conservation Corps in Yellowstone, in the late fall of 1979. I was in this program for a year, and it was a life-changing program for me. I started with an attitude of rebellion and defying God, but before it was over, I changed completely.

We did many different types of jobs in the Park. We

shoveled snow off the geyser terraces to keep ice from forming, cleaned the snow from the cabin roofs, cut down old telephone poles, and rolled up the wire and hauled it to the road to be picked up. Later that winter, I was selected with another man, Kevin, to herd buffalo, to prevent them from migrating out of the Park and spreading brucellosis to domestic cattle. We hiked four miles on snowshoes to a remote cabin in what is called the Black Canyon of the Yellowstone. We stayed there for a week at a time and hiked out at the end of each week.

The job was to push the bison up a meadow about three or four miles. We would whistle, scream, yell, and wave our arms to get the animals to move. We also carried flares in case the buffalo charged, and we always looked for a tree to climb...just in case.

Early every morning, before the sun came up, we would have to get up and light the fire in the wood stove. It was the middle of winter; there was no electricity and it was very cold. We took turns lighting the fire and would climb back into our sleeping bags. When the cabin warmed, we got up, ate some breakfast, and went out to chase the bison. One evening, we were cooking supper when Kevin looked out the window and said, "Oh no! The buffalo are out there, right outside the cabin." We had to go out and push them up the Canyon before dark. The animals were beginning to get used to us and were no longer afraid. We yelled and waved our hands. I don't remember if we lit a flare, but nothing seemed to work. It was getting cold outside and so was our supper. Finally, in desperation, I ran at them with all my might yelling and screaming, knowing they could charge me. There was a tree close by with a large, dead limb within reach. I decided to grab the limb, swing myself out at them and possibly climb the tree, if necessary.

When I grabbed the tree limb, it broke with a loud crack. The noise caused the animals to take off running. I chased them with the tree branch, yelling a special yell that we called "The Buffalo Call." Kevin was laughing and cheering. We chased them up the canyon. When we got them where we wanted them, I let out one final buffalo call. I was getting good at it. Anyway, the ground seemed to shake. Animals were moving in front of me. A herd of elk on one side of the Canyon and a bunch of Big Horn Mountain Sheep on the other were running as well. Kevin was on the ground laughing.

Another time, we walked up the trail and there were no animals to be found. We realized they must have come down in the night, past the cabin, heading for Gardiner. So, we hiked down the canyon toward Gardiner, looking for the bison. We decided to split up. Kevin went up the canyon and I went down. I soon came upon part of the herd, and I called Kevin on the radio to let him know I was moving the buffalo up toward him. Kevin told me he had also found animals and was on the trail above me. I told him to climb a tree. We had forgotten that the entire Park could hear our radio transmission. "Do you need assistance?" we heard over the radio. "Well no, I think we have it under control," I said. Kevin did climb a tree, and it all worked out.

The Y.A.C.C. program had a lot of young people from cities all over the U.S. They were from New York, Chicago, Detroit, Seattle, etc. The program was set up by the government to train young men and women to work.

While I was in the Park, I saw a lot of satanic things. Many were into very "dark stuff." There were Satanists, people into witchcraft, etc. I found out a lot about the dark side and how real God was, and that Satan was real also. Satan tried to kill me, but God spared my life and I came back to the Lord. I was into a lot of satanic things before I went to the Park, but nothing like I saw there. Mother had prayed, led by the Lord, that God would take me so deep into darkness that I would return to the light I once knew. Her prayer was answered, and I did come back to the Lord Jesus Christ with fear and trembling. Dad and Mom prayed often, waking up in the middle of the night to pray for me. It was what I needed.

In 1981, when I left the Park and went back to Big Timber to stay with my parents, I was a changed man. I was overwhelmed by the kindness of people. When I drove into town, people waved and smiled as I drove by, even though I had long hair and looked like a hippie.

I soon found a job with Dave Roys, who had a janitorial service. He also had an airplane and took me for a ride. I worked for Dave until the summer of 1981, when I went to West Yellowstone to work in the Carpenter's Workshop, a ministry to the homeless.

CHAPTER 9
MOVE TO BIG TIMBER

In 1978, Bryan started dating a young lady, Linda Frost. On May 20, 1979, they were married at the Presbyterian Church. Johnny sang at their wedding, and Sylvia and I acquired a new daughter-in-law. Bryan was working at Bozeman Ford. The couple rented a mobile home in a trailer park on Huffine Lane. About six months later, they purchased a mobile home at Hidden Valley Mobile Home Park, where they lived for about two years. In the fall of 1981, Bryan took a job at Gallatin Homes in Belgrade, where they built quality manufactured homes. This was a much better job. Bryan, enjoying his new prosperity, made a down payment on a motorcycle and a Jeep. The next spring, 1982, the employees went on strike. Bryan joined the other employees in the walkout and got his picture on the front page of the Bozeman Chronicle. We don't know if that had anything to do with it, but when the strike was settled, Bryan did not get his job back.

I had co-signed the note for the loan on their vehicles, so we were in a tough spot. Bryan ended up enlisting in the U.S. Army, and I got a motorcycle that I didn't even know how to ride. I ended up selling it to a car salesman in Billings. Bryan completed basic training, then was stationed at Fort Sill, Oklahoma. He moved his wife and son Samuel to Lawton, OK, where Fort Sill is located. His second son, Timothy, was born there. After two years in the Army, Bryan got out and joined the Montana National Guard. He then went to Havre and attended Northern Montana College, where he took a two-year course in electronics. Bryan's daughter, Naomi, was born in Havre.

In the spring of 1980, Forest Supervisor Gene Hawkes called me and said he wanted to take a ride up the Gallatin Canyon to look at a problem summer home. What he really wanted was to talk to me about my career aspirations. I had been on the District for ten years and had not put in for any other jobs, because my kids were in high school and I really was pretty happy in Bozeman, the town where I grew up. Gene was of the opinion that I should have transferred before now. I told him that I hadn't wanted to move while my kids were in school. After our talk, I went home and told Sylvia I thought I needed to put my name in for a transfer. I put my application in for District Ranger, and Gene offered me the Big Timber District, which was still under his jurisdiction, on the Gallatin National Forest. My dad offered us his travel trailer to live in until we found a suitable home, so we accepted the offer and prepared to move.

On May 18, 1980, Mount Saint Helens erupted, and we arrived in Big Timber at the same time as the volcanic ash. It formed a fine dust on streets and cars and was the talk of the day. Dad pulled his trailer to Big Timber, and we parked it in a trailer camp south of town. Daryl Todd was our realtor, and she soon found us a home that was being remodeled to sell. The house was older, but the present owners had added a dormer bedroom, new insulation, and brought all the wiring up to date. The house had a wood-burning space heater that heated the entire house, and there was electric back-up heat in all the rooms. We had to wait to take possession, but it was a nice home. We sold our house in Bozeman for $55,000 and paid $65,000 for the new one. The loan interest on the Bozeman property was 5%, and in Big Timber it was 11%. However, I had my own ranger district and we were happy. Our new home had three bedrooms and two baths. The bathroom off the master bedroom had a telephone right next to the "biffy."

I had attended a lot of law enforcement training, and Big Timber had many problems, which is probably why I got the District. Just before I arrived to take over, someone dynamited a footbridge over the Boulder River at the Natural Bridge. The development was a joint project between the Montana Fish Wildlife and Parks and the U.S. Forest Service, and the bombing was still under investigation when I arrived. There was also a lot of timber theft and poaching of elk for their antlers. The elk horns were sold in Korea as an aphrodisiac.

In the fall of 1980, Beverly started her senior year at Big Timber High School and we settled into our new home. The high school was a short walk, about three blocks. The following is Beverly's story:

The summer of 1980, I stayed in Bozeman with Papa (my grandfather), because I was in driver's training. I would ride the Greyhound bus to Big Timber on weekends until I was through with the training. I was not very excited about leaving my friends and going to a new school my senior year. I remember the day we went to check out the school. I was struck by how old the school building was and the fact that it was so small compared to what I was used to. It was spring, before school had let out. The principal gave us a tour, and when we left, we noticed several of the boys were hanging out of a second story window whooping and hollering. That was rather embarrassing for me.

My senior year, especially in the beginning, was hard. I was very shy, and it was difficult to make friends. Most of the kids had grown up together and lived on ranches around the area. I didn't have a whole lot in common with them. I really wanted to fit in, but I didn't exactly know how. I eventually made some friends, mostly underclassmen.

Then, I started to work at Ferdinands, which was like an A&W root beer stand. It was the first real job I ever had. I made friends with some of my coworkers. The transition from Bozeman to Big Timber was somewhat traumatic for me. It was almost like culture shock, because life in Big Timber was different from anything I was used to. I earned somewhat of a reputation as a "goody two shoes," and I didn't like that image. Of course, art was always one of my gifts and I was recognized for that, so I did all sorts of sports bulletins for the school. I won ribbons at the high school art show, and I did many of the props for the senior play.

I played a leading role in the senior play and was nominated for best actress, but I didn't win. At our planning meeting for the senior banquet, they voted hands down for me to say the prayer. For some reason, I was offended by that and decided that I wanted to fit in with the rest of them. So after graduation, I went to the senior kegger and shocked a lot of them because I was there and was drinking. From that point, I continued to do what I thought would gain acceptance with the crowd. I began to hang out with people who probably weren't the best influence on me, and I was influenced easily at that time. This began some of my more rebellious years. I was rebellious against God and my parents, but I was pretty sneaky and was able to hide most of my newly formed bad habits from my parents.

I really missed my youth group from the church in Bozeman, and during my senior year in Big Timber, I would go with them to different events. I went to a youth function in Lewistown, Montana, and that is where I met a boy named Shawn. We kind of liked each other, and he eventually talked me into applying for college at Oral Roberts University. I also went to youth camp at Hungry Horse, Montana, that August after graduation.

I started working at the Van Cleve Dude Ranch, located in the Crazy mountains outside of Big Timber, right after school let out. I started by helping to open the place before the first guests arrived. After the season got started, they had me come and babysit for one of the guests. I eventually became a cabin cleaner and worked up there all summer, with the exception of one week in August, when I went to camp. I again was influenced by some of the kids that worked up there. I'm not sure exactly where the alcohol came from, but we managed to get our hands on some and did a little drinking at night. After the dude ranch, I got a job working in the kitchen at the nursing home in Big Timber. I saved my money that year to pay for my first year at ORU. It seems crazy that I wanted to go to a Christian college when I was still out doing things I shouldn't have been doing.

I ended up at ORU for the spring semester of '82, and because I hadn't made things completely right with the Lord, I made a lot of poor choices there as well. I didn't take school seriously enough and was too caught up in the social aspects. I had some dating flops and other issues that probably could have been avoided, which caused my self esteem to fly out the window. Consequently, I didn't go back the next year. Instead, I got a job working at Frye's Cafe in Big Timber and moved into a little house with one of my best friends, who moved over from Bozeman. I continued to leave the Lord out of my life and was out partying and doing stupid and reckless things. I'm convinced now that there were some angels watching over me. It was like I had no mind of my own and would go whichever way the wind blew. It was during this time that I met John Gallagher, and when I married him six months later, I still didn't even know him. Things were extremely hard for a lot of years. It wasn't until I realized that I needed Jesus back in my life that things began to turn around. It took many years of seeking God's perfect will in my life, realizing that He had to be first in everything. I had to quit hanging onto my mom and relying on her faith. I had to grow up. Needless to say, Jesus is now my life, my breath, my savior, my guide, my heavenly Father and my very best friend.

In Big Timber, I was approached by the Assembly of God pastor, who asked me to help get a Full Gospel Business Men's Fellowship started in Big Timber. I talked with several people, and after a lot of prayer, we decided to start an independent group and call it the Christian Business Men's Fellowship. We met once a month at Ferdinands Café. Annually, around Valentine's Day, we sponsored a banquet at the Civic Center and invited special speakers, such as Dale Evans, Rosie Greer, and Buz Goertzen, the Idaho yodeler. Most of the Big Timber churches participated.

Sylvia and I also started an intercessory prayer meeting every Monday evening in our home. At times, we had several pastors attend. Bob Shelley, the Episcopal priest, was the most consistent. He and I became close friends and accountability partners. Another close friend and regular attender was Pat Hansen. Several others would come from time to time. We continued to meet until we left for Missoula.

One evening John Gallagher, a young man who had been dating my daughter, attended our prayer meeting. That night, he asked me for permission to marry Beverly. I was flabbergasted; I hardly knew the man. I don't remember exactly what I told him, but I left the decision to Bev. It turned out he had two boys by a previous marriage. I told the couple I wanted them to go to counseling with Pastor Chris Blackmore in Bozeman, and they agreed. Beverly and John were married on November 10, 1984. John had a job in construction at the time, and later he worked as a ranch hand.

The Big Timber Ranger District was the highlight of my Forest Service career. I had good people to work with, including two good secretaries, a geologist, resource assistant, timber assistant and three technicians. I also had several students that we hired in the summer. The district had 347,000 acres, including 182,000 acres of the Absaroka-Beartooth Wilderness. We had 14 million board feet of timber under contract during my tenure. There were 31 grazing allotments and 80 special use permits for various kinds of private use of the Forest, 10 developed recreation sites, 26 recreation residences (summer homes), 5 dude ranches, 4 church camps, and 14 commercial outfitters operating on the District. In 1986, there were 70 applications for mineral patents, and we had a large portion of the only active platinum-palladium mine in the United States.

I presided at public meetings, worked with various interest groups, as well as county and state agencies of various kinds. I enjoyed the work, and in 1983, I attended a three-week training course in forest recreation at Clemson University, Clemson, S.C. In 1984, I was detailed to the Washington office to assist in putting together a special project. It was a good job and I hated to leave it, but the Lord had another plan.

CHAPTER 10
JOHNNY'S ACCIDENT

On Saturday, March 29, 1986, Sylvia and I were visiting with Beverly and her husband in our home in Big Timber when the phone rang. It was Johnny's pastor from Missoula. He told us that Johnny had been in a bad accident and was in the Emergency Room of Saint Patrick's Hospital. I don't remember exactly what details he told us, but we went into shock. After a short time, I called the airport to see if I could charter a plane to Missoula. The airport manager said he would call us back after he had checked the weather, etc. We got some things together and after what seemed an eternity, the airport manager called us back and agreed to fly us to Missoula. I don't remember how we got to the airport. I think Bev and John must have driven us. We boarded a single-engine Cessna and took off. The weather was beautiful and the flight was smooth, but we couldn't think of anything but our son Johnny. I'm sure we were praying.

When we arrived in Missoula, we rented a car and drove to the hospital. Johnny was in surgery and had been for some time. The three waiting rooms were all full of Johnny's friends, people from his church and others. Sylvia and I didn't know but a few of them, and those only in a casual way: Johnny's landlords, Jeff and Pat Smithers; his pastor and wife, Brother and Mrs. Streit; and Johnny's old roommate, Rich Johnson. Most everyone else was a stranger to us.

We waited and prayed. After a while, the neurosurgeon, Dr. Gary, came out. He looked very tired, as he had been in surgery (as I remember) about five hours. He told us he had removed the blood from John's brain, but things did not look good. He told us he could only give him a ten percent chance of recovery. I felt like someone had kicked me in the stomach. Pastor Streit's wife, Dianna, said, "Praise the Lord; all He asks for is ten percent." The doctor gave her a disgusted look but didn't say anything. That evening, the Missoula police officer who had investigated the accident came to the hospital to ask us some questions. He told us about the accident, and we also got information from Johnny's landlord. The following is what happened:

The morning of the accident, Johnny had decided to walk to the grocery store, several blocks from his apartment. It was a nice spring day with temperature in the 70s. He had a backpack to carry the groceries. Johnny had been trained in mobility travel using a white cane, and he made it to Third street, where the store was. He was crossing the street when a pickup, coming from his right in the far lane, hit him. The impact knocked him about 60 feet and resulted in a traumatic brain injury. The accident was witnessed by four individuals, who all told the same story: John was almost across the street when the pickup struck him. Apparently the driver did not see him. A registered nurse was one of the witnesses, and she ran to the scene and took charge. Johnny was unconscious at the scene. He was transported by ambulance to Saint Patrick's hospital, where he was examined and taken to surgery to remove a hematoma (blood) from the brain. He remained in a coma.

We stayed at the hospital until late the day we arrived, then finally went to Johnny's apartment for a restless night.

The next day was Easter, but our focus was on Johnny. We got up and dressed and went straight to the hospital. People from John's church were there, and they gave us a meal ticket to the hospital cafeteria. They also brought doughnuts. The church was like one big family, and Johnny was very much a part of them all; consequently, they were mourning and dealing with the accident like it had happened to a real blood brother. Sylvia and I sort of felt like we were competing or something. Anyway, the church people couldn't do enough for us. They offered to house our family, and if we indicated we wanted to eat or anything else, they would jump in and try to pay for it. I know they meant well and really felt bad for Johnny, but I finally had to ask them to back off, as we felt smothered by kindness, and we needed some privacy. They immediately responded to our wishes. Really, they were great. All we needed was to get some "air." I felt bad about having to say something to them, as we were indebted to them for all they did for us.

Bryan, Bruce, Bev and her husband, John, all came on Easter Sunday. They too were traumatized, as they all loved their older brother. Bev said, "I went in to see Johnny and he was all hooked up to all those machines and it just didn't seem real." Bryan was in his last year at Northern Montana College. He took a week off from school to be with us.

Just prior to the accident, while we were still in Big

Timber, I had completed training in the Dale Carnegie course. Two points of the course were "always show honest, sincere appreciation for other people's kindness," and "never criticize, condemn or complain." The course was fresh in my mind, so I told Sylvia that we should thank John's caregivers and always be positive. She agreed, and we began to practice that with the nurses and others. We made a point of thanking those who cared for Johnny, and many nights we would buy a pie and take it to the hospital for the nurses' coffee break.

As soon as I could, I phoned an attorney friend in Bozeman, Mark Bryan. I remember telling him I needed him. He got right to work and sent an investigator, Mark Tyers, to get all the information he could. Mark had my son Bryan, and John's mobility instructor Del Addis, re-enact the accident so he could video it. He also got a copy of the police report and interviewed all of the witnesses. It turned out that the man who hit Johnny was retired on a disability. He lived in a trailer house and owned an older pickup, the one that hit Johnny. I didn't want to sue him, but I did want to collect his insurance, which was only $50,000. It was some time before the case went to court, but we did collect the insurance. Mark Bryan got a third, Johnny got a third, and Medicaid got the rest because they were paying for Johnny's medical bills. Mark Bryan helped us set up Johnny's money in a trust account to be used for anything Medicaid didn't cover. We will always be grateful for the excellent work our attorney did for us. Later, when Sylvia and I became involved with the Montana Brain Injury Association, I became aware of many problems with property and finances due to or related to brain injury, and I appreciated Mark Bryan even more for the thorough way he handled Johnny's situation.

One day, shortly after the accident, our son Bryan left us and went by himself up Pattee Canyon. He stayed by himself to pray and think. On the way back to town, he picked up a University student who was hitchhiking. The student invited Bryan to his apartment, and they watched TV together. Meanwhile, we were frantic, thinking something had happened to our second son. He had lost track of time, but he showed up eventually. He just needed to be alone.

Sylvia's mother came about a week after the accident. She flew in from Mobile, Alabama and stayed with us in John's little one-bedroom apartment. That was difficult for me, but I think she was a comfort to Sylvia. There was lots of stress for all of us.

I prayed and asked God why this happened, many times. He never answered that prayer. I got very familiar with the Book of Job. Church and Christian friends became very special.

Missoula, Montana is the headquarters or Regional Office for Region One of the Forest Service. At first, they temporarily detailed me to work with my former supervisor, John Drake, who was head of Recreation. Later, I was permanently assigned to Planning and the Big Timber District got a new ranger. I appreciated the Forest Service placing me in Missoula, where I could be near Johnny, but I did not feel comfortable in the Planning job. The department head mostly ignored me, and I didn't have a real position. I tried to keep busy doing whatever I could find, helping other staff, etc., but "Beggars can't be choosers," and I was grateful to be near Johnny. 1988 was a big fire year, and I knew the Chief of Fire Management, so I called him and volunteered my services. He checked with my supervisor, and I transferred to Fire Management for the rest of my career with the U.S. Forest Service.

One day not long after Johnny's accident, I got a phone call at my Forest Service office. The charge nurse, Judy Gerkin, told me that Johnny was having breathing problems and to come immediately. I ran the few blocks to Saint Patrick's Hospital. When I got to John's room, his pastor was there, Sylvia and her mother, the third floor chaplain, a Catholic nun, and the nurse who had called me. Nurse Gerkin said, "Let's pray." She immediately started praying a very Spirit-led petition for Johnny to start breathing on his own, and he did. We got to know Judy and started going to her church, Christian Life Center. We got to know many of the nurses personally and were even invited to one nurse's wedding.

John remained at Saint Patrick's Hospital for about two months. He was then transferred to Community Hospital, under the care of Doctors Bertrand and Stone, who were Physiatrists or rehabilitation doctors. John's recovery was gradual. We were never sure when he came out of his coma. At Community Hospital, he received physical therapy, speech and occupational therapy. On August 18, John was discharged from Community and placed in Wayside Nursing Home. However, he continued to go to Community for therapy and a couple of times was admitted for physical complications.

Sylvia and I eventually moved into a bigger apartment. Sylvia's mother returned to Alabama and immediately broke out with shingles. For a break, I got Sylvia to enroll in the Dale Carnegie course. When she completed it, she went through another session as a graduate assistant. We got very involved in the church and were asked to lead a singles Sunday school class that met at the Sizzler Steak House. Single folks came from several different churches, but mostly from Christian Life Center. Sylvia spent most of her time with Johnny, and I would join her when I got off work. Our kids came as often as they could. My father and stepmother visited often, as well as friends from Big Timber and Bozeman.

In the fall of 1986, Beverly got pregnant. When she went to the doctor in Big Timber, he told her he could hear two heartbeats, and that she needed to be under the care of a specialist, so she moved in with us in Missoula. Her husband, John, was working for a construction company, building logging roads. He worked out of Missoula but was away from home during the week. Beverly gave birth on June 12,1987, to a baby girl, Amee, and a boy, Isaac. John was away when they were born, so Sylvia and I took Bev to the hospital. Sylvia and I helped take care of the babies the first year. The whole family was excited about the twins. My father bragged about them to all his friends. There was no history of twins on either side of the family. My dad enjoyed telling people, "I've researched it and can't find any history of twins in our family, but I did find a couple of uncles with split personalities." I think the babies were a gift to get Sylvia's attention off of Johnny. They were, and still are, a special blessing.

I retired from the Forest Service in December 1988, after 28 years in the Department of Agriculture, Forest Service and four years in the Navy for a total of 32 years of Federal service. After I retired, I volunteered to finish a book on the 1988 fires that I had been in charge of. The book, like a high school yearbook, was about the fire season of '88 and was to be a gift to over 10,000 Forest Service employees who had come to Region One to help with one of the worst fire seasons ever. I saw the book to completion.

During the spring of 1989, Sylvia and I planned a singles retreat at the Assembly of God Church Camp near Hungry Horse, Montana. We had several people attend from all over the State, and the retreat is still held annually as of this writing.

At some point during our stay in Missoula, I became involved with the Montana Brain Injury Association and was elected to the Board of Directors. Scotty MacLeod and his wife Ty, from Billings, were the founders. They had a son with a head injury and worked hard to get an organization started in Montana that was affiliated with the National Association. I had attended a couple of conventions while we were still in Missoula.

CHAPTER 11
RETIREMENT

In June 1989, we moved back to Bozeman with Johnny. We rented a U-Haul truck for all our belongings, and the day we arrived at my dad's home, my stepmother Phyllis, my dad's wife, passed away from cancer. Fortunately, we arrived just in time to be there for him.

Dad was a "snowbird." He spent his winters in Mesa, Arizona, where he owned a travel trailer that was permanently placed in a trailer park. At his invitation, Sylvia and I moved into Dad's home in Bozeman until we could find other arrangements.

We got Johnny placed in a nursing home on North Fifth, just a few blocks from Dad's house. There were other young people with brain injuries there, and the manager was trying to get a portion of the facility dedicated to serve the needs of people with head injury. We were impressed with the staff and asked them to recommend a doctor for Johnny, which they did. Dr. Pamela Hiebert became Johnny's physician, and Sylvia's also.

We got involved with the Bozeman Chapter of the

Brain Injury Association, and since I was on the Board of Directors, I volunteered to host and chair the next conference. I spent the first few months planning our next convention, which I was determined would be the best one we ever had. We had several good speakers, including Montana's Attorney General, Mark Racicot, who later became our Governor, and Montana Senator Max Baucus. We also had a pig roast with a German band playing while we ate. It was great, but I went over budget and we didn't make any money. However, we made some important contacts, which helped us get some legislation passed in the Montana Legislature that benefited our cause. Sylvia and I chaired the Bozeman Chapter of the Brain Injury Association for several years, until she got sick, which I will talk about later.

When our conference was over, Sylvia, Dad, and I took a 7,000-mile road trip to the east coast and the southern U.S.. We drove to Clarissa, Minnesota, where Dad was born in 1907. We also met some relatives in Egan, then drove into Michigan and looked up one of Dad's cousins. From there we went to Harper's Ferry, where my great-grandfather was born. We also visited the Civil War battlefields of Antietam and Gettysburg, and then went on to Washington DC, down through Virginia, the Carolinas, Georgia, and Alabama, where we visited Sylvia's relatives and went fishing in the Gulf of Mexico. From there we went into Arkansas and Missouri, saw more relatives, and came back home. We were gone about a month.

In 1989, Beverly and John Gallagher were working on a ranch near Two Dot, Montana. Bryan had graduated from the Havre Vo-Tech program, and he was working in Bozeman for a biomedical electronics firm that maintained electronic equipment in hospitals and doctors' offices around Montana. Bruce was the custodian for Longfellow elementary school in Bozeman.

In the fall of 1989, Sylvia and I started an intercessory prayer meeting in our home, similar to the one we had in Big Timber. We met once a week, sang some choruses, then took prayer requests and prayed. Ted and Betty Lange, Steve and Claudia LeCoure, Janet Hasbrouck, and Theresa Vogel were the most consistent attenders. Others came occasionally. We met every week for about twelve years, even after we moved to Belgrade.

I also started driving school bus in the fall of 1989. The busses used to collect around the Emerson School. My bus was the first in line on Babcock, and it was my job to monitor the sidewalk along Babcock from Third to Fourth Avenue. I had to be sure the kids lined up and did not go into the street until all the busses arrived. The students on my bus lined up on the sidewalk leading to the front door of the Emerson School, not along a street. When everyone was loaded, the end bus driver would give the OK on the radio and I would lead off, heading east on Babcock.

One day, just as I was pulling out, one of my students came running across the playground waving his arms. I had to turn on my red lights to load him, which held everyone up. The student had never given me any problems before, but he was a different sort of child, and the other kids tended to pick on him. On this particular day, he had decided to go and play, to avoid the hassle of being teased. When he climbed on the bus, I told him I would have to give him a conduct notice (green slip), which the students had to have their parents sign and return for any infraction of the rules of conduct. The boy took his seat, and I glanced at him from time to time in the mirror. He was quiet and very thoughtful. As we got closer to his stop, he said, "John." I answered him, and he said, "You have a really good Christmas, OK?" When I let him off, I said, "Are you going to line up correctly from now on?" He assured me he was, so he didn't get the green slip after all. I guess I'm just an old softy.

The school kids' dogs got to know the school busses and frequently would meet the bus at the stop. One beagle was consistently at one of my stops, and he would whine and wag his tail when his master got off the bus. One day, the student's mother picked her son up at school to take him to a dental appointment. When I got to his stop the dog was there, but when his master didn't get off, the dog raised his head and howled in disappointment.

After two years, I was switched from a regular route to a special ed bus with a wheelchair lift. Teddy Kingma was my attendant the first year. Our route took us out Highway 191 to the mouth of the Gallatin Canyon, then back to Cottonwood Road and up Cottonwood to Hyalite, then down Nineteenth to Bozeman, eighteen miles one way. I had as many as six students, two in wheelchairs. My wife Sylvia worked as an attendant on another bus. The second year, Teddy quit and Sylvia became my attendant.

In the summers, I drove bus for Gray Line out of West Yellowstone, Montana. We took passengers through Yellowstone Park, to Virginia City, Montana and to Jackson Hole, Wyoming on day trips. I would drive and narrate as we went, so I had to read up on the history and geology of Yellowstone and the surrounding area. As a forester, I was fairly familiar with the flora and fauna of the area—at least enough to get by.

In January, 1995, my dad contracted pneumonia and went to the hospital in Scottsdale, Arizona. The doctor told us that if we wanted to see Dad, we should come immediately. My brother Earl and I left right away, and we met our brother Ken in Pocatello, Idaho. Together we drove to the hospital in Scottsdale. We all had an opportunity to visit with Dad for a couple of days, but Earl and Ken had to get home, so I stayed with him. Shortly after my brothers left, Dad passed away while I was sitting beside him. He was a great guy, good father, grandfather and good husband to three wives, two of which he outlived. I put together his eulogy and read it at two services, one in Mesa and one in Bozeman. He was a great influence on me and my brothers and our families. Sylvia and Bryan came to Mesa for the memorial service and took me home. Dad is survived by his wife Doris, who is living in Bozeman at the time of this writing (2008), and is still in good health at 98 years.

In the spring of 1996, I quit bus driving to take a job at the Evangelical Free Church. My title was Assistant Pastor, but I was more of an administrative assistant. I wrote job descriptions, coordinated the construction of the new wing on the south side of the sanctuary, did some counseling with people who had problems and tried to help them using scripture. I conducted half a dozen weddings and a similar number of funerals, including one for my friend Roy Walton, who I talked about earlier. I also helped with the kids' Awana club, started a senior ministry called "Prime Timers," and tried to do things the other staff didn't have time for.

Beverly and her husband John worked on the ranch at Two Dot from 1988 to 1990, and then John enrolled in the Junior College at Trinidad, Colorado to study gunsmithing. In 1994, they moved to Jasper, Alabama, where John worked in a sporting goods store. Bruce had been custodian at Longfellow elementary school, but he had resigned in 1992 and started doing construction work and other odd jobs. In 1995, he went to work at Bozeman Deaconess Hospital, where he worked for several years. Bryan worked for Jordan Biomedical Electronics in Bozeman until the business was purchased by Columbus Hospital in Great Falls in 1989. Bryan went to work for Columbus Hospital when they bought the business, but was stationed in Butte, Montana from 1989 to 1993, when he was transferred to Great Falls.

In 1996, Johnny's nursing home in Bozeman started pulling some things that we didn't like, and we became very dissatisfied with the service, so we transferred him to the Livingston Convalescent Center until there was a vacancy at the Gallatin Rest Home. The Livingston facility was fine, but we had to drive 25 miles to visit him, so in December of 1998, when there was a vacancy at the Gallatin Rest Home, we jumped at it and moved John once more. The new facility was the fifth nursing home for John. Many of the staff had known him from working in the old facility, and we were very pleased with the new arrangements.

I continued to work at the church, and in the fall of 1998, I received a flyer offering a trip to Israel for $800. This included air fare, hotels, and meals. They offered the same deal for a spouse at an additional $1200. As I read the flyer, I went to the kitchen and asked Sylvia if she wanted to go to Israel. She replied, "Oh sure, why?" I told her about the deal I was looking at, and she asked me if I was serious. I assured her I was. We ended up taking the trip of a lifetime.

Sylvia had been having pain in her back, so before we left she got a prednisone shot in her back, which seemed to work, as she made the trip without complaining.

We departed Bozeman on January, 29, 1999, and flew to Minneapolis to connect with the rest of our party. From there, we went to Amsterdam and arrived in the middle of the night. We waited at the airport until daylight and boarded a KLM flight to Tel Aviv. We flew at 35,000 feet, and even at that altitude, we could see the Alps. We marveled at their size. When we got to Tel Aviv, we waited at the airport for everyone to clear customs, then a bus took us to a luxury hotel on the Mediterranean coast, overlooking the ocean. The room had complimentary mineral water, flowers and fruit. We had a private balcony overlooking the beach and the water. The next morning we had a huge buffet breakfast, with lots of fruit, salad, fish, and eggs, but no pork products, of course.

After breakfast, we loaded our suitcases and boarded a bus for our trip up the coast, but first we visited the ancient city of Jaffa which is now a part of Tel Aviv. From there, we traveled to Caesarea and spent time touring the old coliseum and other ancient ruins that have been excavated by archeologists. We then went to Mount Carmel and Megiddo, viewed the Valley of Armageddon, then went to Cana and Nazareth, and finally to Tiberias on the Sea of Galilee. Again, we were in a luxury hotel for the night.

On the third day, we boarded a large boat and went out on the Sea of Galilee. When we got to the center of what is actually a lake, they stopped the engine and our guide pointed out where Jesus fed the five thousand, preached the Sermon on the Mount, and where He cast the demons into the pigs. It was awesome. I felt like I needed to pinch myself, it was so surreal. We drove through the Golan Heights and visited the ruins of Caesarea Philippi, Capernaum and back to our hotel at Tiberias.

The fourth day, we went to the ruins of Beth Shan, the city of Jericho and on to Jerusalem, to our hotel that was to be home for the rest of our stay. In Jericho, Sylvia got to ride on a camel. We visited all the sights of the ancient city, the Temple of the Holy Sepulcher, the Wailing Wall, Temple Mount, Garden Tomb, and the Upper Room where the Last Supper was held. We took a side trip to Bethlehem, Masada, the Dead Sea, En Gedi, and on the Sunday before we left for home, we went to church at the Garden Tomb chapel.

The last day, we boarded the bus to Tel Aviv airport, where we waited for what seemed like hours before boarding our flight. Seated close to us were a Muslim man and his wife, who was covered in a black cloak that extended from the top of her head to her toes, with two slits for her eyes. Her husband had on blue jeans and a tee shirt. I told Sylvia I was going to go ask him how he knew he had the right wife. She panicked and grabbed me. I really wasn't going to do it, but I had to tease her to break the monotony of a long wait. When we got to Amsterdam, it had snowed and a plane had skidded off the runway, so we had to circle for an hour. When we landed, our Northwest Airlines flight had waited for us, but of course, our luggage didn't get on board. It took ten hours to fly from Amsterdam to Seattle, where we boarded a Horizon Air flight to Bozeman.

Our luggage came the next day. Sylvia had collected several Ziploc bags of salt from the Dead Sea, so when they x-rayed her luggage, they had to open it to see what white crystals were in her suitcase. It was a wonderful trip, and we felt safe the whole time. I recommend the journey to everyone.

CHAPTER 12
ALS

Our next venture was a trip in the summer of 1999 to Grand Junction, Colorado to attend a surprise birthday party for my former boss, Bob Cron. We also went to Mesa to see my stepmother, Doris, and on the way home we visited the Grand Canyon. It was at the Grand Canyon that Sylvia fell for no apparent reason. Her ankle just gave way. I helped her up, but that was the beginning of our next trial. Sylvia had more spills and difficulty controlling her ankle, so we went to an orthopedic surgeon in Billings. They operated on her ankle and put four titanium pins in it for support. They also prescribed physical therapy. We have a good friend, Karla Edwards, who is a physical therapist, so we went to her.

On January 7, 2000, my daughter Beverly gave birth to our grandson, Matthew. On January 14, Sylvia and I flew Northwest Airlines to Birmingham to see the new baby. Sylvia had to have assistance, so every time we changed planes, someone met us with a wheelchair. When we got to the Birmingham airport, there was nobody to meet us. I called Bev on my cell phone and she told me her friend, Pam Williams, had Amee and Isaac and should be there to meet us. I went to the information desk and had them paged, but they didn't hear it, or understand it, or something. Finally, I decided to go to the Delta concourse on a hunch. Sure enough, there they were waiting for the Delta flight to come in from Atlanta. We loaded the car and drove the forty miles to Jasper. Bev's neighbor, Mary Long, found a wheelchair for Sylvia to use while we were there. We only stayed five days with Bev, but Sylvia got to hold her new grandson.

On January 19, we rented a car and drove to the Mobile area to visit Sylvia's mother, who had Alzheimer's disease and was in a nursing home. We also visited with her two brothers and their families. We returned to Bev's on the 21st and the next day flew home.

When we got home, we continued with the physical therapy. Karla worked with Sylvia and finally said, "Sylvia, I don't think I'm doing you any good."

We went back to the surgeon, who told us something else was going on. Sylvia needed to go to our family doctor and have a complete physical. We returned to Bozeman and scheduled an appointment with Dr. Hiebert, who gave her a complete physical and ordered us to see a neurologist. Bozeman's neurologist couldn't see Sylvia for six weeks. We shared our situation with another doctor friend from our church, Dr. Len Ramsey, and he told us that with our permission, he would see if we could get in to see a friend of his in Billings, Dr. Williams. We had a phone call the next day from Dr. Williams's nurse, who asked if we could get to Billings the next morning. It was early March, 2000.

Dr. Williams took Sylvia's walker away, put her in a wheelchair and ordered an MRI for 11p.m. Sunday night, the earliest we could get in. When we went to the building that housed the MRI, the only ones there were the custodian and the technician. Her MRI was clear. On Monday, Dr. Williams told us Sylvia had ALS or Lou Gehrig's Disease, that there was no cure, and they didn't know what caused it. Sylvia started crying, and I had a sick feeling in my stomach. The doctor gave us a prescription for a medicine called Ryluteck It was supposed to slow the progression of the disease. Before we left Billings, I called my pastor, Chris Blackmore, and told him I would have to resign from the church to take care of Sylvia.

When we arrived in Bozeman, I went to the pharmacy at Walmart and asked them to fill the prescription. They had never heard of the medicine and had to look it up. When the pharmacist told me it would cost something like $700, I told him I needed a second opinion and phoned the Blue Cross Pharmacy's 800 number. They hadn't heard of it either, but when they looked it up, they told me it would be $35 for a three-month supply. I immediately ordered the drug.

We listed our home in Belgrade with Brenda Witmer, a friend from church, and she quickly sold it for a good price. We then made a down payment on a condo that was still under construction. Some more friends, Ron and Micki Huisenga, owned an apartment complex and offered to rent one of their units at a reasonable price until our condo was finished.

We continued to have our prayer meeting on Monday nights, at Ted and Betty Lange's home, until we moved into the condo. More people attended, to pray for Sylvia.

The day we moved, a bunch of people from the church,

some of my family, and Daryl and Stan Todd, friends from Big Timber, came to help. Sylvia couldn't do anything, and I didn't need to do anything but look after her. Our friends packed us up, moved us and unpacked. The only problem was that I had trouble finding some things later. They were wonderful, though, and the few inconveniences were pretty minor. Ken LeClaire, the contractor who built our condo, was very good to us. He changed his schedule to get our unit built first, because of Sylvia's disease, and he did us several other favors as well.

One day, shortly after we moved, they discovered mold in our crawlspace. We had to leave for a day so they could fumigate. Cindy Ramsey took us for a drive up Hyalite to pass the time. When we returned, the condo had a very strong chemical smell. The only place that didn't smell was the bedroom, so we just went to bed. Cindy and Len Ramsey, and Sam and Cindy Nelson, came with the high-school youth from our church and serenaded us from our bedroom patio.

Our friends were wonderful. We had a steady stream of people bringing us food, coming to pray with us and showing lots of Christian love. The ladies of the church started coming to the condo on Sunday morning to hold church for Sylvia. They would bring their musical instruments and gather in our bedroom to worship. They wouldn't let me stay; I had to go to church, which was a nice break, but I also was curious about what the ladies were up to.

Bev came with the baby on March 29 and stayed until April 5. In June, she came again and stayed seven weeks. Her husband, John, drove the family to Montana, and they helped us move from the apartment to the condo.

Sylvia's brother Donny came from Alabama in August, but he had to get right back, so he only stayed three days. When he got home, he sent his wife Peggy, who stayed three weeks and cooked for us. She went home in October but came again in November, before Thanksgiving, and she stayed until December 15. She brought fresh oysters, packed in frozen shrimp, in her carry-on bag. On Thanksgiving, she made gumbo in addition to all the traditional Thanksgiving fare.

Other visitors were Sylvia's brother Mike and his wife Charlotte, and also her cousin Mildred. While they were here, they helped with cooking and household chores. It seemed like there was always someone in our guest bedroom, but that was good

In October, Sylvia went to the hospital to have a peg tube placed in her stomach, to help with feeding and taking medications. Our friend from church, Cindy Aune, works at the hospital as an R.N. in Day Surgery. She took me aside and suggested that it was time to get Hospice involved. I talked to Dr. Hiebert. She wanted to discuss it with Sylvia, who agreed. Her comment was, "I want to do whatever makes it easier for John." She never stopped thinking of others, even when she was in great pain and discomfort. Hospice started coming three days a week. When they were present, I would go for a long walk.

When our condo was under construction, I had the builders make several modifications to accommodate a wheelchair. We had the doors widened and a special carpet pad installed that would not show the indentations of a heavy wheelchair. We had the end of the kitchen counter lowered so Sylvia could eat from her wheelchair. We also made major modifications in the master bathroom. It was designed with two sinks. We had the cabinet under one sink left open to facilitate the wheelchair. Instead of a tub-shower combination, we had a walk-in shower built that was six feet by four feet, and the shower had a flexible wand instead of a regular shower head. When I gave her a shower, I would use a power lift with a sling to move her from her bed to the shower chair. Then I would wheel her into the shower, and I could get in with her, fully dressed, and bathe her with the shower wand. I got a little wet, but not very.

I kept all of her medications on the counter in the bathroom. I would use a mortar and pestle to crush her pills and put them in her feeding tube. She had a hospital bed and an air mattress that was on a timer that would rotate her from side to side to prevent bed sores. We placed a baby monitor on her pillow, so I could hear her when I was in the kitchen or living room. My bed was right next to hers, so I could care for her in the night, as needed.

Sylvia got progressively worse and about the first of April, her breathing became more labored. I phoned all the kids and told them the end was near. Everyone started to arrive. Bev flew in from Alabama on April 3, and her husband John came the next day. Bryan went to the rest home and got Johnny and brought him to be with his mom for the last time.

At 11:45 p.m. April 8, 2001, a saint went home to be with our Lord. I was beside her when she passed. When I was sure she was gone, I called the kids, who were mostly sleeping in various places in the condo, and told them their mother was gone. I then called Hospice, and they took care of everything.

We had her cremated. On April 16, in the morning, we had a graveside service with just the immediate family and close friends, to inter the ashes. In the afternoon, we had a celebration of her life at the Evangelical Free Church. There was standing room only; someone estimated that over 400 people attended the service. Cindy Ramsey, Sylvia's prayer and accountability partner, planned the service. Dahl Funeral Home made all the other arrangements. My son Bruce sang a special song, written by his friend Elijah Mann.

EPILOGUE

Our family experienced many trials, but mostly we grew closer to the Lord who created us all. Through every trial, we learned more about why God created us and what the purpose of life is. In the Bible, James chapter 1 verses 2, 3, and 4, it says: "Consider it all joy, my brethren, when you encounter various trials, knowing that the testing of your faith produces endurance. And let endurance have its perfect result, that you may be perfect and complete, lacking in nothing." At first, I had difficulty with that verse, but now I understand it.

I have come to believe with all my heart that life is not about us; it is about God. We were created by Him as eternal beings, to live forever. He gave us a free will, which is the freedom to chose whether to follow Him or not. I believe that God created us for at least three reasons: fellowship with Him, fellowship with other Christians and good works.

Jesus said, "I stand at the door and knock. If anyone hears my voice and opens the door, I will come in to him." Is He knocking at the door of your heart today?

I've learned that sometimes our prayers aren't

answered, and sometimes they are answered in ways we don't understand until later. God says, "My ways are not your ways." He sees the big picture, and sometimes he disciplines us or has a different plan from ours. Our lives are interwoven with so many other people that having our way might interfere with what He is doing with someone else, or He wants to use us in a special way. The old gospel song says, "We'll understand it better by and by."

I believe that the short life we live on this earth is preparation, or training, for eternity in God's heaven. Since coming to the Lord when I was 38 (I am 75 as of this writing), I have witnessed His miracles, seen answered prayer, and I've heard His voice. Our God is awesome. When Sylvia was sick with ALS, in the advanced stages, she was bedridden. A friend, Karla Edwards, would come every week and do range of motion exercises on her arms and legs. It was a chance for me to get out of the house for a few minutes. One day when she was with Sylvia, I decided to run to the grocery store, but I couldn't find the checkbook. I looked in all the usual places but couldn't find it anywhere. Sylvia told Karla to have me look in my desk drawer. I never kept my checkbook in my desk drawer, but when I looked, there it was. My desk was in my office in the front of the house. Sylvia was totally bedridden and couldn't possibly have known, except the Lord told her.

The Bible says, "Love the Lord your God with all your heart, mind, soul and strength, and your neighbor as yourself." I have to pray for His help to love some folks, but He does help me. He certainly loves us.

All of my children, Bryan, Bruce, Beverly and John, are

walking with the Lord, largely due to the trials they have experienced, which have been elaborated on in this book.

My son, John E. McCulloch, is fifty years old as of this writing. He has been in a nursing home with the head injury that left him quadriplegic since he was 29. He has been blind since age one. His mind is sharp, he has a solid relationship with the Lord, and he is at peace with his circumstances. He has favor with his caregivers because he thanks them for all they do for him. He seldom complains. Usually, if he gets irritated, he raises his right arm, a reflex action that occurs when another patient is hollering and the attendants are slow attending to the problem. He has never been married. Johnny's hope is in Jesus' promise of a new life, with Him, in eternity.

Today, people with homosexual tendencies insist on the right to exercise their desires, even though the Bible is obviously against it. People are practicing sex outside of marriage. Divorce is running rampant. The philosophy of today's world seems to be, "If it feels good, do it." However, God is the same yesterday, today and forever. He does not change His standards to adjust to the times. We need to let God make us in His image and quit trying to make God in our image. That may take some sacrifice, but it is worth it.

We need to fellowship with other Christians, to be held accountable and to support one another. A good, Bible based-church is the best way to do that. I believe that the church or denomination is not as important as the Christians who attend. Church, in itself, does not save us. We must be born again. In other words, at some point in life, the sooner the better, we need to pray and accept Jesus

Christ as our Lord and Savior. If you have never done that, why not do it right now? You may kneel, lie prone, sit in a chair, or whatever, but bow your head and pray the following:

> *Lord, I am a sinner.*
> *Today, I want to accept you as my Lord.*
> *Would you please forgive me for the following sins:*
> *(name them if you wish, or just ask Him to forgive you)?*
> *From this moment forward, I want to serve you*
> *with all my heart, mind, soul and strength.*
> *Please help me to be the person you created me to be,*
> *and help me to overcome*
> *those things that are not pleasing to you.*
> *In the name of Jesus Christ, Amen.*

If you prayed that prayer, congratulations! The Bible says the Heavenly host rejoices with every sinner who prays to receive Christ. Today, your name has been written in the "Lamb's Book Of Life" that is talked about in Revelation. You can grow as fast as you want to. Find a good church, and get involved in a small group or Sunday School class. May God bless you!

Finally, if you or a close family member are going through a trial today—no matter what it is—please trust God to help you through it. Let Him "Refine You In The Furnace of Affliction."

PHOTOGRAPHS

Sylvia when I first knew her.

Sylvia at home in Coronado, California.

John and Sylvia's wedding.

John gets his Navy wings. Official U.S. Navy photo

McCulloch children, front: baby Beverly,
back row, left to right: Johnny, Bryan, and Bruce.

Bryan and Johnny at Grandma's house.

Baby Johnny

Baby Johnny at Knots Berry Farm.

Johnny at high school graduation.

Beverly

Johnny, giving his graduation speech.

Bruce and wife, RieAnne

Bryan in National Guard uniform with daughter Naomi.

Johnny and Grandpa McCulloch.

John and Sylvia.

Johnny and Sylvia.

Sylvia and John in Israel.

Sylvia, after ALS has progressed.

Evangelical Free Church youth serenading on our patio.

CPSIA information can be obtained at www.ICGtesting.com
Printed in the USA
BVOW031510080112

280064BV00002B/1/P

9 781432 737856